GREEN BARS

An American Bomber Pilot's Personal Story, 1942-1945

Eugene G. Cowart

Recalled and written 2006 for my children, grandchildren, and great-grandchildren

High Flight

Oh! I have slipped the surly bonds of earth
And danced the skies on laughter-silvered wings;
Sunward I've climbed, and joined the tumbling mirth
Of sun-split clouds— and done a hundred things
You have not dreamed of— wheeled and soared and swung
High in the sunlit silence. Hov'ring there,
I've chased the shouting wind along, and flung
My eager craft through footless halls of air.
Up, up the long, delirious, burning blue
I've. topped the wind-swept heights with easy grace .
Where never lark, or even eagle flew
—And, while with silent lifting mind' I've trod
The high untrespassed sanctity of space,
Put out my hand and touched the face of God.

—JOHN GILLESPIE MAGEE (AMERICAN PILOT OFFICER, RCAF, DIED
AGE 19, MID-AIR COLLISION, ENGLAND, 1941)

CONTENTS

BACKGROUND

This will be a war story, my own, to give those with a little idle time and maybe a passing curiosity some insight as to why I am the way I am. This would be in the time of my life before I knew you (and indeed, for some of you, before you were), and therefore before you knew me. I'm sure you have heard most of my stories before. And in some of what is written I have repeated myself. Just deal with it I'm 82.

Like others my age, I have had several previous lives. Or so it seems for as we look back many of our experiences are so vastly different as to qualify as a "Previous Life." And indeed some can almost be considered to have happened in some vastly different parallel universe. (I sometimes wonder if it's still there and still going on. I have, maybe, somehow escaped into the present. Some postulate that there are numerous parallel universes. Current exotic mathematical theory validates this concept and takes it out of the realm of science fiction.) In my case by the time I was 21 and having had a marvelous childhood, I had been a college student, a soldier, flown the ocean, and seen much of the Century's holocaust that was World War II. I find myself sometimes wondering did all this happen or is it all imagined. And if it happened what was my involvement.

> As we stir the pools of memory,
> Memories ripple to the top,
> In wide increasing circles,
> That never seem to stop.

Fortunately (or unfortunately as the case may be) I have a pretty good memory. Especially of signal events in my life. The unfortunate aspects run counter to my mother's adage that in order to forgive someone, one must forget Sadly, while I may forgive someone, I will damned well remember the causative event. That's the way I am.

World War II started September first, 1939 when Germany invaded Poland. This brought France and England in due to treaties. Italy came in with Germany and before long Russia and Germany partitioned Poland. Later Germany invaded Russia (big mistake). We were not directly involved until Japan bombed Pearl Harbor in Hawaii on December 7th, 1941. I was a Sophomore at Auburn. We declared war on Japan and the German axis. In some ways World War II was just a delayed continuation of the first World War of 1914-18.

This will tell you the war as I remember it, along with some prewar background. I am writing this at age 82 and while some things are sharp in my mind although admittedly some may have faded. But all here is true as I remember it. There are no heroics on my part, no tales or blood and carnage. In the air you only know the result of tragedy as you seldom see the blood up close. But to watch a bomber fall is terrible enough, knowing the frantic activities of the crew as it falls. You count parachutes. I was at most a dot or period on the page of a long novel. The novel "World War II" depicts a large grinder with millions involved, and millions lost, on all sides.

Sadly I could never tell stories sufficiently grim to suit my mother's taste. She having been raised on Civil War stories featuring Uncle Louie where little bits of flesh rained down after someone was hit by a minie ball. Allegedly he plunged his sword into a creek bank to keep the Yankees from capturing it along with him. (No word as to why he chose not to use it to kill Yankees.) Everyone involved has a story. She raised me (and later on occasion David and Jan) on made up stories of the pirate Black Shirt Henry and his bloody tales of piracy where the unfortunates were drowned like rats. Mom was tough. She had four brothers, and I, being an only child, was told early and often that I was not to be tied to her apron strings. In fact she told me, although in a loving way, that I raised you to leave. She could, if need be, help my stories. One picture I had of an old French house that had been destroyed by shell fire or had just fallen in she billed (to her friends) as my quarters that had been bombed. Taking her at her word (to leave) I felt free to enlist in the Army in World War II to be an Aviation Cadet.

But before that, a little family history is in order, inasmuch as we're all the sum of our experiences. Or as Elizabeth Goudge said in her novel *Green Dolphin Street,* "We are the way we are because of the places life puts us, the people it rubs us up against, and the things we don't get." Or close to that. I am remembering that from many years ago.

But the family history. My father was born in 1892 in Wallace, Alabama, which is still there, but not much to it, where a railroad passes just north of Atmore. My mother was born in Moss Bluff, Texas, which we laughingly called a suburb of Liberty, Texas. My father's father Daniel Webster Cowart—he said "Danel" D-A-N-E-L, just like the man with the dictionary, which is of course not right since that's Noah Webster—was born in 1854 and lived to almost 90. My grandmother, Margaret Jernigan, was born around Ferry Pass, Florida. We're not sure where my grandfather was born. These are my father's parents.

My mother's parents were born in Louisiana and later lived in Texas. They were Evelyn Sanders and George Francis Smith. My mother was one of six children, and her father died when she was quite young, apparently two or three years old, and with one younger brother. Her only recollection she says of her father— this was down in the southern part of Louisiana—was watching the people at his funeral dip water out of the grave in order to put her father's casket in the ground, which is sort of macabre. I knew my paternal grandfather and grandmother quite well since they lived with us quite a bit, sometimes a source of conflict between my mother and my grandmother, both of whom were rather strong-willed. My mother's mother had a rather interesting life. She was engaged to be married to a young fellow by the name of Burr, Roland Burr—Rolly Burr—who was a descendant of the Burr that shot Hamilton. But he was in Medical School at Tulane when it was discovered that he had tuberculosis, and this was back before the turn of the 20th century. At that time that was a death sentence and the family said no way could she marry him. So he left Tulane just as he finished, moved out to Arizona and New Mexico, and lived out in the open for about two years, didn't die, and recovered. In any event, he was no longer interested in medicine, but moved on to California and spent the rest of his life as a Conductor on the Southern Pacific Railroad. I always wondered how many people, as he was taking tickets on the railroad, realized there was an MD taking them. In any event, he married and had three children and his wife died. And by then he had learned that my grandmother, "Evvy" Evelyn Smith (Sanders was her maiden name), had been widowed. Rolly carne back to Louisiana and got my grandmother and married her and they moved to California. In time all of Evvy's children moved to California with her, with the exception of my mother Carrie Fay and the oldest boy, Clifford, who had disappeared by that time. He went off to work somewhere in the oil fields and was never heard from again. This was about the time of World War I.

With that little background I can move on into some of the other things in my earlier life. I was born in the large city of De Quincy, Louisiana in 1923, and as an infant moved on to Birmingham where my father worked for a short time before, as he said, "got fired from one outfit." And then we moved to Pensacola where he spent the rest of his life. Now my father was a graduate in Architecture from Auburn in the class of 1913 (or Alabama Polytechnic Institute it was named at that time). He said he tried architecture for a little while and walked the streets of Mobile trying to make a living, but said there was too much of a requirement to be a joiner, and he wasn't very good at that. So about that time World War I carne along he enlisted in the Army. He served in France in the 7th Infantry Division and came home unscathed. He never had any really great war stories. Apparently he spent a good bit of his time as a water tester (benefit of a college education) riding around in a motorcycle side car, although he was in an Infantry Division.

I had a very happy childhood in Pensacola and still consider it my home town. In my early childhood I was bad to run away, so my mother said. I would take off at the drop of a hat and they'd have to run me down. Later in life, a little bit later when I was in the first grade, my mother was desperately afraid of thunderstorms and used to walk around in the house in Pensacola with a pillow on her head, which has nothing to do with anything, but I saw this. It marked me, as I could understand later in life what mental illness must be like because when I was in the first grade, if a cloud passed over the sun I had the most terrible feeling of dread, and if not restrained would run away to go home. On one occasion, knowing that if I got home I would be brought back, I went miles downtown to my grandmother's house. And just as I got there she drove up—my mother did—and back I went to school. This passed after the first grade. But I do remember that feeling of dread when a cloud would pass over the sun.

There were only a few things that I always could do well in life

—I was sort of a skinny kid, fairly smart in school, but I could whistle, roller skate, swim, body surf, and, later in life, fly formation. These few talents were hardly those which would foretell greatness. And they didn't.

I finished high school in 1941 and went off to Auburn to study engineering. Although my father had a degree in architecture, he always worked as an engineer. I stayed there about a year and a half. I was in the Army ROTC in the Corps of Engineers there, but the war started long about then and I decided I wanted to be in it. I wanted to fly. But before that they had a recruiting campaign. And I still remember a fellow by the name of Fowler, who later became a Judge in Alabama, Conrad (Bully) Fowler—came in in his Marine dress uniform and almost recruited me to go in the Marines. However, once my father was visiting there and we watched an airplane fly by and I made the statement, "Boy, I'd give ten years of my life to do that." My father looked at me and said, "By God, I'd do it then."

So with his blessing, I left and went home to Pensacola, went down to the Post Office to enlist. I wanted to be in the Navy since that was a big Navy town. And in the basement of the Post Office there was a recruiting office. When I went into the Navy office there was a bunch of papers to fill out, and also to write a one-page autobiography—maybe 100 words or so—which really didn't sit too well with me because I didn't like English. With that I went around the corner to the Army Air Corps—same papers, but no theme to write. So I joined the Army Air Corps in November, Friday the 13th, 1942, and away I went from there. I was one month past my 19th birthday.

(As an aside, I had walked off from Auburn being young and stupid I suppose, and really didn't clear out properly). When I tried to get back into college after the war, I had all X's and had a terrible time convincing anybody I really wasn't stupid and hadn't flunked out. I did finally get in, but I went back to the University of Alabama instead of Auburn. I always said that after being a Freshman at Auburn that World War II was nothing.

My travels led from Pensacola as follows: Miami Beach,

Florida-Galesburg, Illinois-San Antonio, Texas-Coleman,Texas-Greenville,Texas-Frederick,Oklahoma-Shreveport, Louisiana-Lake Charles, Louisiana-Savannah, Georgia-Bangor, Maine-Goose Bay, Labrador-BW1, Greenland-Keflavik, Iceland-Prestwick, Scotland-Stone, England-Toomebridge, Northern Ireland-Great Saling, EnglandBeauvais, France-Wavre, Belgium-Venlo, Holland-Tidworth, England-Southhampton, EnglandNew York City-Camp Kilmer, New Jersey-Camp Blanding, Florida—and home to Pensacola. About 3 years round trip.

The following material concerning stateside training is presented in sequence. However only the first part, recalling overseas assignments, is in order. After Group assignment and combat operations, material is often in random order reflecting what came to mind as I was writing this.

PENSACOLA/ MIAMI BEACH

When we first moved to Pensacola I was about two I suppose. We moved into a place on Devillier Street, which was an ordinary working class neighborhood at that time, not too far from where my father worked. It has now gone downhill. My mother didn't want to tell anybody we'd ever lived there. My father did have one experience there at Newport Industries as he was sharpening his pencil getting ready to climb up on a building that they were working on when it exploded right in front of him. Luckily he wasn't in it, but I remember my mother dragging me and running to the place to find out if he was all right, which was quite a tragedy in the town at that time. Luckily nothing happened to him.

I guess one of my earliest recollections as far as airplanes go— and I had to not be more than four or five because I looked on them almost as little toy-type things up in the sky—but I remember this terrible noise one day, and I realized that two of them had run together. I really didn't know that, but I could see two falling to earth. I was so young that I thought that these were small toys, and I wanted my father to take me over to look at them. I didn't realize that undoubtedly someone had been killed because there were no parachutes coming out of them. That was my first real introduction I guess to even thinking about airplanes.

Another incident that happened was when I was in the first grade that my kindergarten teacher happened to run over me on the way home from school one day. I was walking home from first grade and she jammed on the brakes and hit me and knocked me sky-winding. Instead of taking me home, she insisted on taking me to some doctor's office, who finally decided I was all right. But I remember being terribly sore for several days after that.

We moved around a good bit in Pensacola. Some people kidded and said we moved every time the rent was due, although I don't think that was it. My mother was rather restless I suppose, but eventually we wound up close to Bayou Texar in Pensacola.

Most of my life my major recreational area was around or in the water. We all learned to swim when we were very small. I would guess I learned how to swim when I was not more than five. I was always nonplussed and couldn't imagine people drowning, although some did. I remember we built kayaks, which would probably be about nine or ten feet long and would carry one person. When a new house was being built we managed to make off with some of the lathes. In those days, lathes were used for holding plaster. I think they are no longer used. But they made great structure for a kayak. We covered those kayaks with canvas and then painted them, making them waterproof.

I further remember fishing with my father in the gulf where we'd fish for pompano. And one time after a big flood, I remember out there in the surf—salt water—there were three alligators that had washed out I guess from some lagoon. I remember my father going up to them and poking them with a fishing rod. They were small I guess. I didn't get close. I spent many pleasant hours fishing with him.

Later, when I got to driving age, you had to have a pass to go over the bridge to the Pensacola Casino. Prior to building that bridge, you had to go to old Pensacola Gulf Beach (as they called it), which is still there, but miles away from downtown Pensacola. But to go over to the Casino you had to have a $5 car pass with a sticker on it. A group of us boys would get somebody's car —we were up to 16 or 17 then—and pay the $5. As soon as we drove away we would pull the sticker off the windshield and then whoever could get a car, we would lick that pass and stick it up and pass through that way. This went on for quite a while. We also used to hitchhike over to the beach, and occasionally somebody would let you off halfway there and I can remember standing around on the hot asphalt road trying to get a further ride. I also remember fishing off of Pensacola Bay Bridge with my mother and father one morning, and my mother pulled up a small fish. I still remember her saying, "My God, it's a trout," and threw rod and reel and everything into the water, which caused my father to have a tantrum.

Later, when I was older, another fellow and I were fishing off that bridge at daylight one morning and pulled something out of the water. And just as we did, an enormous shark rolled under it. I remember it rolled him on its back and I can see that mouth now. So if anyone says that there are no sharks in Pensacola Bay, they are not correct.

Another event I recall at the start of the year everyone was telling what an exciting experience they had had the summer before. I remember the Sardinia brothers—John and I forget the, other one's name (Salvatore?)—told their most exciting event was that their father, who worked on a fishing smack (that was a sailing-type fishing vessel that went all the way down to Campeche Banks off Mexico, commercial fishing), had fallen overboard and the sharks got him. Suffice to say, that pretty well killed off any further exciting summer reports. Stopped the teacher cold.

I later had a small sail boat, about 12 or 14 feet, round bottom cat boat rig. I guess I was 14 or 15 years old. We all spent a lot of time in the water on boats. I wanted to be in the Navy since it was a Navy town. I remember overhearing naval officers (fathers of friends of mine) talking and we would be listening to them. I spent a lot of time with Navy children. The officers would talk about how they hoped the Japanese would start something because it would be over in six weeks. In time we all learned better than that.

I had one tragic experience that stayed with me a long time. When I was 12, one of my friends—a boy by the name of Jack Roark, who happened to be the son of the City Manager in Pensacola—died. We were all in a Boy Scout Troop and nothing would do but that we all had to go over to the funeral. I was too young to know what was going to happen, but I remember being led back into a place where there were a lot of ferns and growth, and suddenly there he lay. He had apparently been sick for some time because it was not a very pretty sight. I was horrified and stricken by that. It stayed with me forever, although now I can look at dead people and not think too much of it.

On November 13, 1942, which was a Friday the 13th, I enlisted in the U.S. Army at old Ft. Barrancas in Pensacola. That was the only time I remember in the Army that we ate off plates. At that time, rather than mess kits, this being an old Coast Artillery Fort, we ate boarding house style. We had big white bowls on the table of whatever we were eating and white plates, I remember, and knives and forks. I believe this was about the last time I ate like this until a year or so later at an officer's club.

One other thing I remember while at Auburn was that an entire Infantry Division passed through town right after the war started. It took two days to pass and it was hard to get across the street. I became serial number 14057379 (and you always had to remember that), and that was my enlisted serial number, the "1" meaning that I had volunteered, the "4" meaning I was from the 4th Corp Area, which was the Southeast. Ft. Barrancas was, as I said, an old Coast Artillery Fort, and prior to the war people might spend their entire enlistment there occasionally firing the large guns that defended the harbor. Occasionally they would bring in railway guns back of town and shoot over Pensacola at targets in the Gulf. All parades were always led by an old fellow with a horse who had been at that Fort forever, Captain Jack-something he was called, and well known around town.

Shortly after enlisting, I was on a train to Miami Beach for basic training. It seemed that Roosevelt had met with Stalin and Churchill, and said, oh yes, he could put a lot of people into the service, and he did. Although I had enlisted to be an Aviation Cadet, it turned out that I was sent in as a Private like many others and I actually spent quite a while as a Private in the Army. We rode the train, as I say, to Miami Beach and were subsequently quartered in a place called the Rendale Hotel. This was fine, except that the elevators were not allowed to run and we were on about the 12th floor. So it was up and down the stairs when you fell out or fell in, but it did make for good sleeping as you were well tired by day's end. I was in a room with three Davis boys, all not related, but named Davis, a fellow named Cullen, and myself. Mainly drill and exercise is what we did. We had one little short regular Army Sergeant—a Tech Sergeant as I recall—not very tall and he required everyone to wear his hat sort of peaked on his head like him. The only time I've seen that in the Army. But he had a terrible temper, and I guess it was necessary to deal with us. One of his favorite sayings was he was going to make us sweat our outline on the wall. That was always, "I'll make you sweat your outline on the wall." We also had a drill instructor from West Virginia—a real hillbilly—named Barker. I can remember him saying "gentmuns, get your feets in line." He could also tell all kind of stories.

We also at that time got four shots at a time. I can remember you would line up and there were always Filipino soldiers that gave whatever kind of shots they were, four at the time. In fact, right after one series of shots, we got up at daylight the next morning and double-timed over to a theater to take some tests. I'm surprised we all passed for those of us that did as it was hot, close and we felt like hell. Poorly lighted too. It was necessary to make a passing score to qualify for officer training. Some didn't.

The drilling we did was with old Lee-Enfield World War I British rifles. Mine seemed—I was about 6 foot tall and 140 lbs—like it weighed 200 lbs. and almost sawed a hole in my shoulder. I further remember the mess halls that we ate in. Here we were eating in mess kits. We had a bunch of Corporals and Sergeants always yelling "Eat it and beat it. Drop it and mop it." You could be so tired during drill periods that when you got a ten minute break (every hour), lying down on the ground and going sound asleep.

Also, some of the hotels were civilian at that time, and next to the place where we cleaned our mess kits were big garbage GI cans full of hot soapy water. When we weren't doing that we'd climb up the wall and ogle old men and young girls in the hotels next door (to everybody's chagrin on that side I'm sure). Another humorous thing that did happen featured our evil-tempered Tech Sergeant. All of the blinds in the hotel, (being military), were to be at the same angle, elevation, and attitude. Once out in the back when we'd fallen out, I remember the Sergeant looking up and one had blinds flying out the window, flapping in the breeze. The Sergeant immediately threw a fit and demanded to know whose blinds those were. I remember this little redneck fellow by the name of Boyce from somewhere in rural Alabama, complete with a real accent, he stated, "Them there blinds belong to Boyce, and if the Newnited [sic] States Army don't like it it's just too bad." I thought the Sergeant was going to just shoot him right there.

Another event I remember was we were in khakis—and although it was Miami Beach and you'd think it was warm, it was down around freezing, and we all had khaki uniforms on. We had a big parade and review, and way out in front I could see this staff car come up. Pretty soon, some officers, brass, about four of them got out with overcoats on, stamped their feet around, got back in the car, and left. By then we had about frozen to death. Another introduction to the Army.

I was, as I said, a rather slim kid like some of us were. We had this physical training instructor—sort of a real jock-type guy, part thug and a real physical specimen. He was famous for grabbing some skinny kid to demonstrate one of his judo holds and tie you in a pretzel. This happened several times. So we decided to fix him. We had one fellow in there with us by the name of Sager from Birmingham an ex foundry worker—a real solid type. This instructor called for volunteers and this time we sort of propelled Sager out into the circle. The fellow without really thinking tried to get a hold of Sager and do something to him, and it was just like grabbing the wall. I remember finally Sager just threw him down. That was the last time he called for any of us skinny kids. I don't remember what happened to this instructor after that, but Sager was our hero.

COLLEGE TRAINING DETACHMENT (CTD)

I finally finished Basic Training in Miami Beach after much exercise, marching back and forth, getting shots, eating out of mess kits, in the company of eat it and beat it, drop it and mop it, which I've mentioned before. And finally they issued us wool uniforms —at least an overcoat and wool uniform, and put everybody on a train. Not really knowing where we were going, but we were going. As stated earlier sometime in late '42 or early '43, Roosevelt met with Churchill and Stalin, with Stalin pressing mightily for a second front. And Roosevelt said, well he could bring a lot of people in in a hurry in the Army and he did. I was one of them.

I had enlisted to be an Aviation Cadet, and ordinarily I would have started at that rank right off. But to bring in a lot of people in a hurry they brought us all in as Privates, which I was for some months before becoming an Aviation Cadet. On the train we were all put two in a lower berth, one in an upper berth, and shipped off to we knew not where until the train stopped in about three days. Not really knowing where we were, we finally were told it was Galesburg, Illinois. As we marched along I can remember some brick streets. It was also very cold—I don't know, January or something like that. I had on an overcoat and I had my hands in my pockets. This tall Sergeant yelled at me, "Get your hands out of your pockets," which of course is a no-no. When I got them out he saw that I had no gloves and he said, "Okay, put 'em back in."

We marched across town to Knox College and were put up for the night in a college dormitory. By this time it was snowing pretty good and here was a Florida boy who had never seen snow, except maybe on a mountaintop way off from a train. As luck would have it I was selected to walk guard duty the first night (I think from 2:00-6:00 or something like that). The other fellows in the dormitory there had come in from Jefferson Barracks, Missouri, and they were from that part of the county. When they saw how few clothes I had, they outfitted me with what was really cold weather stuff (more layers). I was then sent out and given a walkway or place to keep marching back and forth around the dormitories equipped with a wooden rifle. I always told everyone though it was very successful as no Germans or Japanese broke through my line at Knox College.

I should say something about Knox College. I had been going to school at Auburn, studying engineering and had been there about a year-and-a-half when I left and joined the Army. However, getting to Knox College was something new because it was a small liberal arts college, and a rather nice one. Supposedly it was the original old Siwash, and was said to have had the cornerstone laid by some President way back in the 19th century. (Benjamin Harrison?) They had very nice dining hall facilities, much better than the average Private in the Army ever saw. And in addition, they had a library, which was really a beautiful thing. It had separate rooms for the books, and nothing the library at Auburn or what I saw later at Alabama, or for that matter any other large university could compare. Fireplaces in some rooms.

This then was what was called a College Training Detachment or CTD. When Roosevelt made good on his promise to Stalin they took this mob in, some had been in college and some I'm not sure even had a high school education. We were to be there from 2-5 months taking various kinds of general courses, some math, history, geography, and things of that nature. Being in my second year in college, I wasn't there but two months, which was long enough. I also didn't stay in the dormitory but a few nights, and after that they marched us across town to an old YMCA and we were put two to a room in an old seven- or eight-story YMCA building. Went through Galesburg a year or so ago and it's still

15

there as an apartment.

This was pretty well presided over by two Sergeants (there were officers around in charge of everything but Sergeants were our face of the Army). One of which was about as mean as a rattle-snake, and the other one was a very gentle, almost fatherly, old fellow. I think now as I look back it was probably good cop, bad cop. I do recall that the mean one was always threatening to have someone scrub the floor, which had small octagonal-shaped tiles. He wanted it scrubbed with a toothbrush to be sure that all the black was out of the grout, which was not possible of course. In the meantime, the older, better, easier sergeant was always coming around and making amends for this other fellows bad temper. Actually, I think these were people who were from the old-time regular Army and were really sort of nonplussed and put out by being caught up in a war. At least Knox College was a pretty good location to ride out the war. I think that they wanted to do nothing to get them out of there and into a regular unit.

Our classroom work wasn't too difficult. In fact, it was really not much more than a really good high school education, but it passed the time and wasn't too taxing. We did have to march, of course, occasionally and stand inspection. We had one officer who apparently knew someone named Cowart that he didn't like because he would stop at my bunk and ask my name and then for no reason award demerits. Demerits, when you got them, required that you walk tours depending on how many demerits you had. One hour for each demerit. And that was to walk back and forth with a rifle (wooden rifle here but later as a cadet an old Springfield or Lee Enfield). for an hour and walk off your demerits. These officers, tactical officers, were ground non-flying officers in the Air Force and were pretty much administrative for handling people like us. I felt sad for some of them that I saw in Miami Beach that were going through an Officer Candidate School because they were obviously older and out of shape. I hated to be near them when they were running because I knew that one of them was going to have a heart attack or drop dead from the exercise, although none did while I was there.

One thing that worried me a great deal while I was there, however, was a meningitis outbreak amongst the soldiers. One of the fellows had passed out and I helped to get him to sick bay, and all the time him breathing in my face. At the time I didn't realize that he had meningitis and was later concerned that I might contract it. My concern was not as much about getting the meningitis as being left out of the class, being left behind, and having to start over. But, no meningitis, and I did get through the coursework. and ship out on time.

One nice feature of being there, however, was that it was a very friendly small town that had never really seen soldiers around there like we were. And it was very easy to get a free meal. The main thing to do was to stand on a street comer, and in our case speak with a broad Southern accent. Immediately you were taken in, brought home, and treated like a king. One family I remember took me in and fed me and then took photographs, some of which I still have. The man was an amateur photographer, but a very good one.

I also probably came as close to getting killed there as any time during the Army outside of combat. I was down near the depot, where there were two parallel train tracks. I was watching a troop train going through in one direction. It had all kinds of artillery and tanks on it. It was on the second rail. Just as it passed I was about to step out when another train—a very fast passenger train (the Zephyr I believe)—was coming through in the other direction. I could not hear it and was facing in the direction of the military train and not looking that way. I could have reached out and touched it. I did not realize that there were people behind me running and yelling. And I couldn't hear them trying to get to me to pull me away from the track. But about one step and it would have been all over because I would have stepped into that train, which was moving through town at probably 50 or 60 miles an hour.

I'm sure we woke up the town, as quite early every morning we had to march from the YMCA over to the College, which was some blocks away. We would sing or whistle as we marched, and we were loud if nothing else. And I'm sure that at 6:00 in the morning or earlier the citizens would just as soon have been left alone.

Probably one of the more interesting or beneficial things that we did in college training detachment at Knox College in Galesburg, Illinois was we did get to do a little flying. This was all in light planes. I flew in an Aeronca. I think we got less than ten hours, and it was primarily riding around with an instructor. There were no landings or takeoffs by us, just handling the controls and learning what the airplane would do and give you the feel of flying. We did some maneuvers or controlled turns and that type thing. The check pilot that I had—the old man was quite old, probably half as old as I am now—wrote me up as having above-average coordination. Finally, after two months, my College Training Detachment was complete. I was again after only two months being put on the train, again not knowing where we were going, but going with the usual two men in the lower bunk and one man in the upper bunk for another trip. As I recall the trip lasted at least three, maybe four days, when we finally wound up in San Antonio. My one recollection of the trip though, besides being bored, was doing KP in a baggage car, with the side doors opened and freezing cold. I remember washing dishes, mess kits, and the cooking utensils in that baggage car, which was a portable kitchen. The doors being open as we passed through St. Louis and snow everywhere. I thought I was going to freeze to death.

My other recollection of that KP on the baggage car that left me with an aversion to coleslaw for many, many years. I recall watching them grind up cabbage and making coleslaw. It was apparent when they cut it open there were very large worms as big as your finger wound around in those things, but they sliced them all up anyway and away it went. Of course, I assume that these worms had eaten nothing but cabbage, which is what they were feeding on. So I guess they all tasted like cabbage. In any event, I did not touch coleslaw until many, many years later, and then and even now I'd take a good look at it.

Aviation Cadet Cowart 14057379

SAACC/PRIMARY

Our next move was to SAACC City (San Antonio Aviation Cadet Center)—referred to as SACK City. During World War II the Army taught flying through three centers: Central, Western, and Eastern. San Antonio was the Central Flying Training Command. The Western one was I believe in Santa Ana or somewhere in California, and the Eastern one was, I believe, headquartered out of Maxwell Field in Montgomery. Not positive of that, but I know there were these three.

We did eventually arrive in San Antonio, Texas, where we spent a good bit of time in the "Classification Center." They tested you and exercised you and decided what your classification would be; i.e. Pilot, Navigator, or Bombardier. Also a more thorough physical exam to determine whether or not you were flight-worthy. There they invented a thing called "Mess Management" It was stated that they needed to teach the new officers to be how to run a mess hall. What it really was, again, KP (Kitchen Police).

One of the first thing that the old Mess Sergeants would do was catch a young fellow and say, "You want to fly? How about flying the China clipper?" Of course, many of the guys said they would like that. What that was was a terribly big, extremely hot dishwashing machine that would scald the hell out of you if you weren't careful, and it was one of the meanest jobs there was.

After watching this for a while, I found there was another KP related task that I got into, almost by accident. I became a G-man, not knowing what a G-man was. But a G-man was a fellow who stayed in the garbage bin (a screened-in place back of the Mess Hall) where all the garbage was sorted. You would sort it out and make sure it got in the right can. This seemed like not too difficult. However, it did have a shortcoming. That shortcoming was that it had to be done exactly right and the cans had to be scalded and washed out thoroughly until you could almost eat out of them. The real big problem was that GI prisoners came around and emptied them and they were usually very mean-looking black men about 8-foot tall. They would walk in and not say a word, and look in the cans. If they were not exactly right as to what was in what can they'd kick them all over and leave. You had to then pick it all up, re-sort it, clean it out, and essentially start over. Of course, I had no intention of saying anything to any of them because they looked like they could probably tie you in a knot before they ate you. Suffice to say, the coveralls I had on would stand by themselves and smelled from a distance.

One thing that did happen that was humorous now, but it was not humorous at the time. The CQ was a cadet temporarily assigned as Charge of Quarters that also lived and stayed in the barracks. He was just one of the guys, but he was appointed that. And his job was to get the KP guys to the mess hall early in the morning at the right time. The right time, was about 4:30 or 5:00 in the morning to be sure everything got ready for breakfast. One time we were awakened, fell out, and taken over there, and it seemed it was rather dark, which it usually was. However, after standing around a good while and nothing happened— nobody was there—we began to wonder what had happened—why the regular Army cooks weren't there. Someone finally got out to enough light to see his watch, and saw that it was about 2:00 in the morning. We then realized we had been brought over there way too early. We went back to the barracks, and no sign of a CQ. We planned to kill him at that time. However, we did have to go back over and wait until about daylight when everyone showed up. We found out later that the fellow's watch had stopped and he was fearful he wouldn't get people there on time, so he sat up as late as he could and then took all of us over there and told us it was time. Then hid.

There were really two parts to SAACC City, or San Antonio. One half was the Classification Center where various tests would determine whether you were going into Bombardier training, Navigator training, or Pilot training. I wanted to be a Pilot, but was fearful that my eyes were not good enough, and wanted to fly for sure. So I put down my first preference as Navigator, Pilot second. Actually, Pilot is what I wanted. When we got through and got classified, I was identified to go to Pilot training, and was elated. This classification business lasted about six weeks, maybe seven weeks, a great deal of which was hurry up and wait, stand around, because they only did so much testing of us. The rest of the time we were more or less at loose ends doing KP and exercise and marching back and forth. This brought out probably the worst of us because we would start singing "the 2nd lieutenants are at it again, winning the war with a fountain pen" to antagonize our Tac officers. We also learned a trick when we would cough—a whole group of students instead of saying cough what you might think, we would cough and say horse manure, except we didn't say manure—we said the real word.

We soon found out that they were taking some of us over to Randolph Field for training new flight surgeons. Randolph Field is an old pre-World War flying field and a beautiful place, permanent buildings and real nice set up. They would take 18-20 of us in a truck over there to be picked and poked and fooled with by these would-be flight surgeons. We referred to them as farmer doctors as they seemed to have come in out of the field. I remember one was giving me some eye tests and thought I was blind until I had to show him how to run the test equipment since I had already been through it three or four times. We soon found out that they always sent more of us than they needed. So I and several others would always hang back and not get selected for playing with the would-be flight surgeons. This left us to run around that field, go to the PX, and drink copious quantities of malted milk shakes, go down on the flight line and look at the airplanes.

The tests that they gave us, in addition to all the physical tests were to determine eye and hand coordination, where you would line up two sticks pulling on strings to be sure you had the right kind of depth perception. They would see if you could hold a pointer in a middle of a ring that it didn't waver and touch the edge .... I know what they were doing—playing what some psychologist thought was the thing to do to find out whether you would make a pilot or not. During all that time we were pretty well confined. None of us were allowed off post or open post, whatever it was called. We stayed on base. We were not allowed to go into town, which is probably just as well, as I'm sure we would have found something to get in to, which would have not been positive.

However, not everything was grim. In preflight we also had these enormous, thousands of cadets on the field doing a review—and somehow I and several others—one friend of mine by the real name of Stonewall Jackson Raley, that was his real name—got to lead this thing. All of us carried a sword and white leggings and we would lead the entire review. But one thing that the Cadet Corp soon got onto—they had a band, and when the band would do rustles and flourishes, or whatever it is, and click the drum sticks, clickety, clickety, click, the entire Cadet Corp would start doing tsk, tsk, tsk all over the field, which sort of set the whole thing off to a big laugh. Not appreciated by whoever we were doing the review for I'm sure.

Once classified we started 9 week Pre-Flight School: largely more classroom work, Morse code and blinker training and lectures on becoming an officer. I believe there was some theory of flight, math as applicable to navigation, aircraft recognition slide shows (outlines of various types of aircraft flashed on a screen). Swimming instruction. This was where I realized that not everyone could swim (I had learned early, as a child in Florida, and I now discovered that some of these guys were from dry inland states). Also training on the Manual of Arms. That was no problem to me as I had almost two years of ROTC at Auburn. A friend of mine by name of Clayton Crunk (from New England somewhere) had served four years in the Marine Corps prior to army enlistment to fly. Real cool dude who suffered fools badly. This sort of fat young Second lieutenant was demonstrating the Manual of

Arms, calling the sling a strap and Crunk snickered and sort of laughed. With that the Lt. said OK wise guy you do it. First Crunk tightened the sling and then went through the manual like dress parade. Sort of stunned the Lt. It didn't come up again. He and I flew together through as cadets from time to time, but we separated after we graduated. The next time I saw him was standing outside my airplane in a place called Camp Lucky Strike in France. Lucky Strike was where they brought all of our returned POWs. Apparently he had been shot down and was a prisoner of the Germans and got back to this place. We had flown down to Camp Lucky Strike in France (this happened much later) to take someone back that had visited us and we had to take him back to where they were being processed. I looked out the window and there stood Crunk, still looking mad as he did when he laughed at the lieutenant. But the thing that I do remember about that, we had gotten one wheel bogged in a soft spot and had these guys there with shovels trying to dig out. I noticed one of them was sort of a tall, redheaded, freckle-faced boy, and I thought, boy he looks like somebody might of gone to Auburn. About that time, this big black guy came up, soldier, with a shovel and hit him in the rear. I realized then that he was a German prisoner and this black Sergeant was running a detail. Sort of a shock to watch that.

We were also subjected to the pressure chamber where they took groups of us up to a simulated 38,000 foot altitude. Not a problem with oxygen masks but hell on a bad tooth. Bad teeth were found out as the low pressure caused excruciating pain necessitating a quick exit from the chamber for the cadet and a quick trip to the dentist. We were also shown how hypoxia affects you. (Lack of oxygen,) One cadet, at altitude, would be told to take his mask off. No problem at first and told to perform some repetitive activity. So far, OK. But when told to stop they just kept on getting dopier and weaker until we put his mask back on. Hypoxia will kill you as you lose consciousness and can no longer function well before you pass out. This is thought to be what happened to one of the cadets I knew that was from Tuscaloosa. Flying a P 51 in Europe he slowly dropped out of formation, no hostile fire, and drifted away. His father came over and talked to me once after the war and he had never been found. MIA.

Finally, the great day came and we were classified—in my case pilot—and I think put on a bus—I don't think it was a train—and delivered to Coleman, Texas to an air base there. A primary flying school. These primary flying schools were dotted all over Texas at that time. These were run by the Army and had an Army officer in command. Cpt. Freedman I believe was in command of this base. However, all of the instructors and the instruction that was done was done by civilians—civilian instructors, civilian ground school, things of that nature. (Ground school reminds me of a cadet by name of VerBeek from Nebraska or the Dakotas. When aircraft engines were being explained he would break in, "yep! yep! just like a Ford tractor." Freedman was a flying officer, but the other few officers on the base would be ground pounder officers who spent most of their time trying to antagonize the rest of us. I can recall one time that was a big joke (to them). They got everybody up about 3:00 in the morning and told us the beds looked bad. Naturally they did since we just got out of them. I guess all this was to make us ready so that by the time we did have to fight it would be nothing compared to training. My flight instructor was a civilian by the name of Coulter. We referred to him as "the knife." I remember a rather slender guy with a little thin mustache and not too old, late 20s. He could really cut you up when you screwed up.

All flight training for a cadet was about 36 weeks—four 9-week periods. The first nine weeks was preflight, the second nine weeks was primary flight training—and in my case the Fairchild PT 19 (Primary Trainer), a low wing monoplane. Second, or basic flight training was in a BT 13 by Vultee (called a Vultee-Vibrator because the way it shook when you did a spin in it). And then advanced, which was either single-engine or twin-engine. For me in twin engine it was mostly in a Cessna AT 17 with a little time in a Curtis AT 9. More about them later.

BT-13 (AKA Vultee Vibrator)

My first flight with Coulter—he flew us around in this plane and let you try the controls to see what it did. I remember (learned) one thing well. He asked me to point at something and I stuck my hand out of the cockpit and almost broke it because of the slip stream. That's one thing you learn very quick—you don't stick your hand out of the cockpit. We would fly by clouds and over and through them and just get a general feeling of the thing before we ever really started instruction. That was the first flight. After that we began to slowly, but surely, learn how to turn, climb, recover from stalls, practice simulated forced landings, and aerobatics (rolls, snap rolls, spins and inverted flight) and most importantly how to start the thing. It took one on the ground to crank the inertia starter to spin up the engine while you flipped switches and controls in the cockpit before taxiing out for take-off on our dirt field.

We flew as cadet in the front seat with the instructor in the back seat. He had a tube going in our ear so that he could talk to us, but you couldn't talk to him. I remember also that in the first part of flight training, the air speed indicator was covered up. That way you were supposed to learn how to fly by feel, and I guess we did. The plane did have flaps that you pulled down with a lever. In fact, I remember the first time that he pulled the throttle on me and that was for me to simulate a forced landing. I just sat there. I thought, well, the engine's quit and he's in the back, he's instructing, go ahead and let him get it down. With that he went into a tantrum, shaking the stick and raising hell in general with me for being dumb, which was true. The Air Force supposedly had a belief in teaching people to fly by pressure all the time. They rode you pretty hard and I developed a pretty thick skin quickly. Because otherwise you'd really be up the creek.

It was anticipated that you would solo in about ten hours, and most of us soloed in about eight. I did it in eight. You were required to wear your goggles around your neck until you had soloed and then when you did solo you could stand up in the mess hall and yell, "hurray, hurray, I soloed today," which was a big deal. There were upper and lower flight classes going through flight school at that time in primary. And of course if we were the ones that hadn't soloed were in the first part. I remember when he finally got out of the airplane and told me that I could solo. The field was divided into two halves where the people soloed—the people like me, the younger people, flying on one side and the advanced students flying on the other shooting landings. Anyway, I took off with no problem and decided that, well, since he's not back there raising hell all the time I'm won't have to watch the altitude so closely, let it get up and down a little, and it was supposed to be held right on. I tried to fly the pattern around the field and suddenly I had wandered off altitude and an advanced bunch of cadets cut me out of the pattern. Not intentionally, I was just out of place (altitude). I had to get out of the pattern, fly off, and then come back in on the far side of the field and land over there. Then, not wanting to take off again and not being supposed to, I taxied all the way back across the field. Coulter, by then, was doing a rain dance out there, and told me that I had to be the dumbest SOB he'd ever run into—probably true.

The author in silk scarf (supplied by photographer and
worn in turn by trainees having their picture taken)

Another little leatherhead I pulled is we had to fly cross country and he went on the first one. It was just a little short thing.
I remember: Coleman to Miles to Bronte, Texas. A hundred or so
miles all told. There's not much out there in west Texas. In any
event, I had memorized the map and everything about it and
thought I was all set. With him riding in the back seat we got
underway. He suddenly asked me something about the map, and
I didn't have a map. Again, a temper tantrum. I'm sure I was not
the only one doing these crazy things, because I have since read
that the flight training going on during the war had about 25,000
accidents—everything from fender-bender-type things to catastrophic.

Speaking of catastrophic, we did have one fatal accident in Primary where the cadet and the instructor were killed. This was
a real bummer-type thing. It was even more so because some
of us (including me) were selected to escort the casket. We had
to be in our Class A uniforms with hats off, and go down to the
undertaking parlor. I can remember them rolling back this big

door and going into this undertaking area—cold, cold, cold, cold I remember. I guess it had to be. The casket was closed of course. (Aircraft accidents tend to require closed caskets.) We had to walk with that casket back through the little town of Coleman with pedestrians standing alongside the procession to the train station where the unfortunate fellow was put on the train for the ride back to wherever he came from. This was sobering and did bring it home to us that this was serious business. In fact, we were told along the way that for every 100 of us they would wash out 50 of us and kill two of us, and that probably carne true because we did have our accidents and a number of them were fatal.

Back to primary flight training. However, I believe we were to have through the whole flight syllabus, primary, basic, and advanced— about 250 hours of flying time by the time we graduated. Accordingly, we must have had about 60 or 70 or 80 hours of primary. After soloing a while and flying a while, you become fairly proficient. And I did enjoy flying that little primary trainer around because it was not too difficult to fly, not too fast. I think we'd cruise at about 120, something like that. And you could do all kinds of aerobatics in it. And we could sign out, and were expected to go out, and pick a particular area and do aerobatics in addition to flying cross country by ourselves.

I remember one rather unusual experience to that I had there. There was one fellow, a friend of mine . . . . Most of us were from garden-variety-type colleges, but this fellow whose name was Louis Stackpole-Dabney was from Harvard. And I remember the only man I ever saw that had a tattoo in the Army. None of us ever got one, but Louis had one on his arm for some reason—some secret society. In any event, his mother visited us in Coleman, Texas and took myself and him and several others out to dinner one night. Dinner in Coleman, Texas is not exactly a big deal, but it was as good as they had. In any event, as I was sitting there—and I had my cadet uniform on—this man came up from another table and put his hand on my shoulder and said—I forget how many years he said, an odd 20 number of years ago—he said I had dinner with Lindbergh this night so many years ago and you remind me very much of him and left. And everybody started kidding me about it. Sort of was a pleasant thing but I thought, my God, I'm not Lindbergh for sure right now.

Another pleasant thing that happened there, we used to play a lot of baseball. That was a lot of fun. There was a family there that pretty well adopted the Coleman, Texas flying bunch, and they used to invite us out to their farm out from town—and we'd go out there for barbecues, picnics. They had apparently been in the circus or a carnival. They did magic acts, with this man and his wife doing all these rather elaborate acts after we got through eating. We built a fire and sat around singing. Really was one of the more pleasant experiences. I do remember though that Coleman had a small square downtown and on Saturdays there was always a bunch of the town loafers squatting around there. . . . Most of us were single; however, there was one fellow by the name of Harry Bush, from Massachusetts who was married. On one of his visits to see his wife he went into town and got to talking to one of these loafers and mentioned that he didn't like Texas. I remember this little fellow looking at him saying, "If you don't like Texas how come you joined our Air Force?" And that's pretty well the way it was. It was referred to as the Texas Air Force at that time.

In the barracks we had double-decker bunks and I had a lower bunk. And I remember very well that in the upper-deck bunk was a fellow from Massachusetts by the name of Valentino Casto-lina from Boston. The main thing I remember he wasn't exactly a handsome fellow. He had severe acne on his face. He had one other problem. He could not wake up. In the morning we would have to almost hit him with a stick because he would invariably pull the cover over his head and say, "I'm up, I'm up, I'm up." Of course, he wasn't and we'd have to get him out in time for reveille.

We also had another fellow, David Cahill I believe was his name, who had a snore that sounded like a B-52 taking off. We used to assign people to keep him awake until the rest of us went to sleep. Because if he fell asleep and started snoring, nobody else in that barracks was going to sleep that day.

There were flying schools all over Texas at that time. And we were told to never fly over another flying school. And one time on a cross country, I had flown the route of the cross country, and on the way back I crossed over the school at Bonham, Texas. I flew right over that primary flying school and did a slow roll and then got scared thinking, well, they're probably going to report me and find out and then I'm really going to be in trouble. However, nothing came of it. But I do remember doing that slow roll right over Bonham. I was pretty high. But nevertheless, I just had to show off little bit.

It was a good experience being mixed up with all these different kinds of people because I was from the Fourth Corps area, which is the Southeast, coming from Florida. Most of us were from Alabama, Georgia, Tennessee, and Mississippi, but we had gotten mixed in with a bunch from the First Corps area, which was New York City, Boston, and the Northeast. It was quite a change because we both eyed each other for quite a while before we finally figured out, maybe the guy is all right. But some of the things that did go on between the two of us. We would argue about the Civil War per ad infinitum.

This was 1943, and of course the war was sort of in a stalemate in Europe and other places, and D-Day of course was not anywhere near yet. So some were, by then, thinking maybe the war would be over before got through there. But sadly that didn't happen.

One thing, previously mentioned, was that the Army was very efficient at giving shots. And as always, invariably, Filipino soldiers. They would give four shots at the time as you walked along. If you stood there they would give your four more if you didn't keep moving. One fellow that we deviled all the time telling him he was going to get a shot, and by the time they stuck the needle in he'd passed out and we'd have to drag him off. This would also happen in these big reviews we had in Texas where it was real hot. Invariably there would be people pass out or fall in the ranks. Of course we'd have to drag them out. And pretty soon we got onto the fact that if you'll pass out we'll get to drag you off and we'll all get out of the sun. But they got onto that pretty fast and made sure that the guy really had passed out. And it never bothered me, but some seemed to go out pretty easily. I found out later that some had found that by putting soap in their shoes and behind their knees seemed to cut down circulation and you could cause yourself to pass out easily.

I was lucky in that I never had to go on sick leave in the Army. In some three years I never really had any reason to go. I did get some good dental work done. Although the dentists, I remember, would work in these little stalls, guys working in their undershirt and spent most of their time squirting water on each other. But I did get good dental care there. Though hardly hard core under-privileged I was at least 15 or 16 before I ever saw a dentist; then without Novocain.

They did have some no good Flight Surgeons. In fact, some of them were real turkeys. We did have one in France later, and I'll describe him later since he stayed most of the time with the bot-tle. It's just as well since I'd hate to have him work on me. He was always telling everybody he ought to be back at the base hospital instead of working on dolts like us.

Primary eventually ended after our nine weeks. They'd washed out a good number of fellows, some due to air sickness—they couldn't overcome it. You'd see the fellow getting back from the flight having a bucket and going out clean up the airplane cause they just couldn't keep from being sick. Others had some kind of problem and never could solo and they moved them back somewhere else to make bombardiers or something else out of them. I don't know, they left us anyway. And we moved on finally and the next stop for me was Greenville, Texas, Majors Army Air Force Base, and that was not a civilian facility.

Solo'd in No. 150

BASIC FLIGHT
TRAINING

I finally survived primary flight school in Coleman, Texas without breaking my neck. I became fairly proficient in the little PT19 with its 175-200 horsepower engine (depending on model). It was a nice little plane to fly around and do aerobatics and pretty harmless I guess, although some managed to kill themselves in them. One of those planes that could just barely kill you. I was then transferred to Greenville, Texas to Majors Army Air Force Base. This is where things got real, because this was an Army field. There were no more civilians running anything. I did hear, however, that Coulter my old civilian instructor at Coleman did eventually get a commission in the Air Force and became a P51 pilot. I lost track of him after that.

In Greenville, Texas we flew the Vultee BT13, the Vultee vibrator. This airplane was about double the airplane the primary trainer was. This was a pretty good sized airplane, about twice as heavy and twice as much engine. This one had a 450-horsepower radial engine with a 2-speed propeller. Another thing one noticed is the control stick in the little Fairchild was sorta like a bicycle handlebar, whereas the stick in the BT13 was like a Louisville Slugger baseball bat. In addition, the BT13 had an enclosed canopy that you could open in flight, but primarily flew with the canopy closed unless you're doing aerobatics. The reason to keep it open then was because it had been known to jam during aerobatics and you couldn't get out if you had to jump.

This was a lot of airplane and we did learn in time to do all kinds of things in it—stalls, spins, snap rolls, vertical snap rolls, and slow rolls, lazy 8s (similar to Primary but more so). We had all Army instructors at this time—some good, some bad, some indifferent. We also spent a good bit of time in the Link trainer, which is a little trainer in the hangar where you sat under a hood and practiced blind flying, where you had to fly a beam and come in over an airport and turn properly and show that you could get down to a landing approach on instruments.

We lived in tar paper barracks, which were pretty cold most of the time. It was either here or later in training that I remember in the winter where it was very obvious we had married up a bunch of us from the 4th Corps area in the south with a bunch of boys from up north in big cities. The barracks had potbellied stoves in them, and it soon became apparent that these boys from up north did not know how to build a fire. Being city boys, their idea was to fill coal in it and then fill paper in on top of it, light it, and hope it burned. It never did, which meant that us redneck hillbillies had to get the coal out and redo it right and then get the fire going.

UC-78 Adv. Trainer, AAFPTS-Frederick, Oklahoma
At-17 (AKA Bamboo Bomber or Useless 78)

At this time in our training, we learned, as I mentioned, aerobatics. We flew on instruments. We learned formation flying, some night flights, and cross-country flights. One humorous thing that happened to me on one flight it had been raining quite a bit the day before. When I took it out and flew it, rolled it, and water fell out of the bottom of it all over me. I thought that someone had used the relief tube in it and had not had the airplane cleaned up. I thought that I had urine all over me, which set me off until I realized it was just water.

However, many things did happen to us in Basic in Greenville, Texas and very few funny. It was serious here and we did have accidents. I had an instrument instructor who I despise to this day, a little sawed-off peckerwood redneck named Lt. Hinton. If there was ever a redneck he was it—a little short fellow (short fellows hate tall people). He would sit inside warming his hands and say, "Cowart, pronounced Kayert you get out to the airplane and sit there till I get there." You might sit out there freezing to death for quite awhile while he warmed his hands inside. Eventually he would come out and stand by the airplane (he could barely see over the edge of the cockpit), look in and say, "You better do good today boy cause I ain't in no good mood." That was for a start. He had other great charm too, like always yelling while you were under the hood doing blind flying. One time he even managed to make me cross behind a flight of B24s, whose propwash almost turned us over. He thought that was hilarious. He was always saying, "Well, I'm gonna jump out and leave you. You're so bad, I'm just gonna leave you in the airplane. And I'll jump." Once when I was flying, it got so quiet that I thought, my God maybe he's done it. I was sitting in the back seat under the hood, and I could see down underneath, and finally I saw candy wrappers coming down. He was up there eating candy. As I lost altitude from looking under the panel at him he immediately went into a rage again. Finally I did survive Lt. Hinton and got out of that phase of Basic flight training.

Formation takeoffs were sort of trying because you were having to watch your airspeed as well as the other airplanes. One of the check rides that I had was from a Lt. Zimmerman. I remember that he took me up and finally said, "Well, just do any aerobatic maneuver that you feel you can do." It had been stormy weather for about a week and no one had flown and I suppose I was a little rusty. I figured, well I'll do a vertical snap roll, which I thought I could do pretty well. I promptly fell out of it and did terrible. Zimmerman said, "Well, if you're willing to even try that I guess I'll figure you're all right," and I got by with that one.

One of the more sinister things that happened to me though was night flying. I was checked out by Lt. Molitor, another gem that I can remember well. We went over to an auxiliary field in the dusk or late afternoon to be checked out for night flying. We made two landing while it was still daylight, and then we made two in the dark while he rode the controls. He then got out and says, "Okay, you got it." By then it was pitch-black dark. So off I went. He had failed to tell me how to turn on the cockpit lights on the instruments. Now an instrument panel has phosphorescent instruments so you can see them if you get down close enough to it, but the best I could do was get my head right down to it while I was on final approach to read the instruments. I was lucky not to have put it into the ground nose first. Somehow I did survive this, but eventually learned about turning on the cockpit lights.

I mentioned the canopy though. It was closed when it was cold, flying around at night. And there, if you had the canopy closed, the instrument lights would light up the inside of the canopy. So we kept it open and almost froze to death.

Another not so funny thing that happened to me with those lights—the BT13 had a rheostat that you control your instrument panel lights. Right adjacent to the rheostat were two toggle switches that flicked on your landing lights with. One night I was flying in the landing pattern and reached down to turn up the rheostat to see the instruments a little better and flicked up one of the landing lights. I immediately thought there was an airplane right on top of me and went zooming off out of the pattern with tower calling, "What's wrong with you? What's wrong with that airplane?" Eventually I got back in and did land.

However, the tower one night—we were all flying in patterns around the field making landings—he yells, "Pull up, pull up, pull up," and every airplane in the pattern pulled up and out. Unfortunately one fellow on final (that the tower was yelling to) went into the trees and burned up.

We had another accident that happened at night when some guy drove into the ground and killed himself. All of us used to sit around and talk, "How could anybody do that? How did that happen?" Well, shortly thereafter I found out how it could happen. We had about four different kinds of night landings stages. One of them was called cigarette butt lights, which you could not see the landing lights on the runway until you turned on final approach. They were supposedly combat lights they told us. I was flying that stage and had turned on final and picked up the lights. The BT 13 had a landing approach speed of 90 mph air speed indicated. If overshooting, you could pull back (slow down) to 80, and cause the airplane to sink faster. The BT 13 flaps were hand-cranked down, ten turns to get full flaps. I was on imal approach and saw that I was going to overshoot at 90 so I'd slowed it down to 80. And seeing I'd need full flaps, I just kept cranking. I hit the stop and sheared the pin off. So then I'm at 80 mph, close to the ground, full flaps, and getting a red light to go around—the ground controller, was signaling I had to go around. I remember jamming the throttles full on, full flaps on, I'm slowed down to 80 mph and the damned airplane wouldn't climb. I went careening out across the prairies on the edge of a stall at between 50 and 100 feet off the ground in the pitch-black dark. I'm thinking, this is how the guy pronged it into the ground. Luckily I finally got a little flying speed and got it up to a little bit higher altitude and came back around, still with the flaps down, and landed. I pulled off to one side and this fellow jumped up on the wing. I looked up and said, "Boy, I sure thought my time was up that time." He says, "What's wrong?" And I told him. He said, "Take my airplane and go back up." Of all the things, it was the damned squadron commander, Lt. Baldwin—a tall, slim guy I remember. I seriously considered saying "Just forget it. I'll get out and you can court martial me." But I sucked it up and took his airplane, went up, and completed the training. I guess it was the thing to do to say get back in the air.

Because that's what I did.

Another accident happened right in front of me. I was in the #1 takeoff position, waiting to take the runway. The kid ahead of me took off and the plane nosed up into the air about 100 feet or going straight up, stalled and fell back on an airplane on the taxiway off to the left and both of them exploded. I'm just staring at the thing there, just dumbfounded. I finally realized the tower was saying, "Take off, take off, take off," and I had to go. But I did see one guy run out of' that big black puff of smoke. I found out later it was a friend of mine, a cadet by the name of Darling who had taken off with his trim tabs rolled all the way back. You had to roll those trim tabs in when you were landing to keep the nose up, but you're supposed to neutralize them and reset them before you took off, and he failed to do that. It killed the fellow that he fell on, a guy from Corsicana, Texas, fell right on top of his airplane. But Darling survived. I remember hearing that he was running along the runway and that two WACs grabbed him —women Army soldiers—and held him down because he was in shock. He did eventually get through flight training and became an instructor. At least I guess he would always instill in the cadets the thing of having their trim tabs set right anyway.

Another exciting thing at Majors Air Force Base in Greenville, was it had two parallel runways separated by, I don't know, a hundred feet or so. We would be flying off of both of them, and when you'd come in for a landing, you would be flying straight at the other guy, except he was going to land on the left-hand runway and you were going to land on the right-hand runway. Occasionally at night a guy would overshoot one and come in on the other runway. Then there were two of you there trying to go down at the same time. That was always exciting. Of course we did have one fellow who missed both runways and landed on the hard stand between the rows of parked airplanes. This was the topic of conversation for a while.

When you fly you usually keep up with what we called the spread. This was the difference between the temperature and the dew point. Because if the dew point and the spread come together, fog forms almost instantaneously. I had a check ride once with a Major that I didn't know. I was little bit apprehensive of it, because I remember him having sort of a "look down your nose" mien, a beautiful flight suit big leather jacket and some really colorful flight boots. I figured he might be difficult. In any event, we took off on sort of a cold and rainy day like that. We had hardly got off the ground and only a few hundred feet in the air when fog started forming, almost instantaneously. The spread had gone together. He had mentioned it might be close. He merely said "Never mind, I got it," and took it and flew us back and we got back in almost as the field was closing. In any event, he said, "Well, we'll take this up later." I never saw him again and it was all right with me.

A lot of cartoons then were showing a cartoon guy named Dilbert who showed all the dumb things cadets did. And all of us did a lot of them. That's where the phrase "head up and locked" came from where you had your head stuck up your rear end and it was locked up in there and you didn't know what in the hell you were doing. That's how some of us killed ourselves.

I remember some of the leatherheads that I pulled. On one cross-country flight I was doing cross-country to Paris, Texas to land, and I remember as I looked down on final and thought, "Boy, it sure seems like I'm high." And sure enough, as I started down I realized I was only 1000 feet too high. I had miss-set the altimeter. On another occasion on a cross-country flight, across Texas, I remember landing at Mineral Wells, Texas. When I landed I saw they had what looked like light planes. They were really L5 liaison planes the Army used for artillery spotting. One of them took off, and as he did he pulled straight up. I thought, God here's another one like the one I saw that crashed in front of me. However, these planes had the power to do that. About that time, whoever was running the field tower called and wanted to know, "What are you doing here? You don't belong here." I then realized I was on the wrong field. So off I went, keeping that to myself—I don't think I reported that—and finally got to the field I was supposed to land on. We had to land at different fields and takeoff and do round robin cross-country.

At this time, we also got quite a few talks on flight safety. One I can remember very well because the fellow instead of having on brown shoes had sort of a yellowish pair of shoes. And he was a Major or Lt. Colonel. I think they overdid it because they were telling us that, "You realize that if you crash it will be a mess. And the casket we send home will just have a uniform in it and bricks in there because there won't be enough of you left to weight it. So we have to weight it down." Don't know if that was true or not, but that's what they told us. And when you're 19 or 20 and in a situation like that you believe damn near anything.

It was while I was at Majors Field in the winter that I remember getting word that my grandfather, my grandmother, and uncle died within a few months of each other that year. (My Dad's whole family and I'm sure it was a strain on him, that with his only son off in the Air Corps.) There was nothing I could do about it other than getting a call to come over to the office or headquarters and get a telephone call from my Dad telling me what had happened. Weather was pretty miserable at Greenville, Texas at that time of the year, which was winter. I think it must have been around Christmas, the best I recall. But I do remember flying around at night. They would send us up in twos separated by 500 feet altitude up to 5000 feet i.e. 2 at 1000, 2 at 1500, 2 at 2000 and on up to 5000. Then they'd call us down two at a time in 500 feet increments to make landings. That's where those lights in the canopy would bother you and you'd keep the canopy open and it'd be so damned cold you'd freeze flying around up there. One time, I was at 5000 feet and was right at the bottom of some clouds. I had kept running in and out of them, which made for a joyful experience. Not.

But eventually, in time I did get through and we did graduate and finish basic flight training, in the old BT 13 which was really a pretty good airplane. Sort of fun: to fly after you got onto it. We could fly all around over the country on our own. I remember flying up on the Red River in North Texas. At that time, we were divided up. Some of us were sent to twin-engine flying school and some to single-engine. Not really knowing how it carne about, nevertheless, I was sent for twin-engine flying school. At the time I thought probably I was too tall for singleengines. Too big to get in the cockpit, which was probably doubtful. But it seemed to be one of the things we thought. As I said, kids at that age will believe most anything anyway.

ADVANCED FLIGHT TRAINING

Basic flying school at Majors Field in Greenville was finally completed. It was determined that I would go to twin-engine flying school for advanced training. Of course, all of us thought we'd start out being fighter pilots or something, but twin-engine wasn't bad since that could lead to some other interesting situations.

I was transferred to Frederick, Oklahoma for twin-engine school. It was quite a town. I remember it had one stoplight in the middle of town with a bell on it, to be sure that if you couldn't see you could hear it. The field was a typical wartime field. There were tarpaper barracks, which were rather unusual in that they were all anchored down to the north and open to the south. I hadn't been there very long when I realized why this was so. It was the coldest place I think I ever was. It was flat apparently all the way from Oklahoma all the way to the North Pole, and the snow blew all the way up to the eaves on the north side of the barracks, and we could only get out to the south.

It was another time when the Yankee boys from the cities still could not build a fire in a potbellied stove. As I think back, they may have been intentionally dumb, and we were too dumb to know it. In any event, those of us who knew what we were doing could get a fire going, because otherwise I think we would have frozen.

The aircraft we were using here most of the time for training was a UC78 or an AT17— same thing—referred to as a "bamboo bomber" by some of us. It wasn't a bad airplane and fairly easy to fly, twin engines, I think 245 hp engines or 295—I forget which. I spent a lot of time with instructors becoming familiarized with the airplane. It was a really rather forgiving and easy to fly airplane. It wasn't particularly fast or anything. Some people referred to it as the "useless 78" instead of the UC78.

At this time, we did a great deal of night flying, cross-country flying, and instrument flying. We were really beginning to home in on this type of thing. We originally flew with one instructor. and two cadets—one cadet sitting beside the instructor and the other one sitting in a back seat. One of the jokes that was played on people was to be out late at night and hit the alarm bell. Usually the guy in the back was about half asleep and immediately thought he had to jump out. Luckily no one ever did from that particular position, because it would have been difficult.

Once we got to fly the airplane, we flew two cadets together, swapping off whether one would be copilot and one would the left-seat first pilot. We did a thing there that I didn't do anywhere else in training. That was that we would fly one morning, be off that afternoon, fly all night long, first half shooting landings, and the last half would be cross-country or night formation flying. Then the next day we would reverse that and be off in the morning, fly in the afternoon, off that night, and then fly again the next morning, off that afternoon, fly all night long. And this went on all the time in an attempt to either speed things up or to be sure we got as much time as we could.

I soon found out flying at night that part of the country—Oklahoma and Texas—pretty well went to bed at 9:00. Because if you were expecting to see a town down there after 9:00, it was all lights out and nothing to be seen. Surely they rolled up the sidewalks or whatever they had. The thing I remember at that time, at night, we were doing either dead reckoning or flying by light lines where there'd be a red light stuck on a pole, which gave a code sign. And if it was an airport it had a green light with the code sign. The trick was to always read the light first. Because if you decided what light you were looking for you could invariable see that particular light. And it was not pleasant to get lost over West Texas or Oklahoma at that time of the year or at night. We also used to say that we thought that Oklahoma and Texas were the two most air-minded states in the nation. This was because of the dust storms that they would have. One day all of Texas would fly into Oklahoma, and then next day Oklahoma would fly back into Texas—a lot of red clay dust. Very unusual though. You could be at 10,000 feet and could look straight down and see the ground, but you could not see very much ahead of you.

With fellow trainee Robert S. Crooke

Before two cadets set out on the cross-country flights at night, we were to work up the plan where we were going, headings, timing, and all the things you would have to do to plan a cross country flight at night. I had always worked mine up, and usually the people I flew with worked their plan up also. We did have one hotshot-type cadet though that I remember very well that was not too well liked. He and I got assigned to fly together one night. We hardly got in the airplane when he said, "You got your stuff worked up haven't you? Because I didn't have time to do mine." This was a lie, because he had plenty of time. However, not liking that situation I said, "No, I didn't work mine either." This was a lie. I should have told him that I had, but I didn't. In any event, we took off sort of by main strength and awkwardness and seat of the pants piloting, flying across this West Texas country at night. I was in the left seat flying while he should have been navigating. By the grace of God and I don't know what else, we did finally get around after flying some hours and get back to the field. However, just as we were turning on final approach I looked down when the fuel indicator light came on, and we were running out of gas. We did get down on the ground. But it taught me one thing, that regardless of what kind of a jackass you got in your airplane with you, you better be sure that you got your stuff ready. And I never made that mistake again.

Naturally a bunch of young guys flying around at night by themselves, and having radios there, there was some foolishness that shouldn't have gone on. But somebody would get on and say this is the Green Hornet, and somebody would say something else to them, and pretty soon your instructors would be—if they were anywhere in the area—yelling shut up, and when we find out who that is we're gonna bust you out. And of course they never did.

There was a movie that came to the theater called *The Desert Song*. Pretty soon you had guys all across the cross-country singing "The Desert Song" at the top of their lungs. Don't know what would have happened had we really needed the radio. We'd be all strung out across Texas and Oklahoma carrying on like that.

Another humorous thing, in Frederick, Oklahoma—of course gasoline was pretty well rationed—there was one beer joint we used to go to that had been a filling station. And one acquaintance of mine was a boy from Mattoon, Illinois by the name of—I don't know what his real first name was—Nose Pearson (for obvious reasons). We were in one of this beer joint one night and a rather healthy-looking, middle-aged barmaid was serving beer. Nose Pearson got about three sheets in the wind and when she bent over to serve the beer, he reached up and grabbed her right on one of her adequately generous hooters. I remember her looking at him and saying, "Why young man," and hauled off and knocked him clean out of his chair. Suffice to say, that was the end of Nose Pearson's romantic escapades.

We had two instructor pilots assigned to a crew of—I forget— four or five or six cadets. We had a Lt. Goodman and Lt. Plant. Plant was from Florida and not a bad guy to deal with, only he was a little proud of himself. Whereas Goodman was bad news as far as not putting up with any foolishness. He was a tough instructor, but a good instrument instructor. Since I had a fairly thick skin, they would try to get me to fly with him first to see how bad he was, which I did because I had got where I could pretty well put up with anything. Yelling and carrying on didn't bother me too much. Once this friend of mine named Crunk, though, that had been in the Marines did something one day and Goodman told him, "Well, you're no better than the Nazi German." And I thought they were gonna come to blows. Luckily they cooled down, or he cooled down, and everything went on all right after that.

Most of the instruction was in AT17s, the bamboo bomber. There were also on this field a certain number of AT9s, which were also used for instruction. All of us got some time in an AT9. An AT9 was an all-metal little twin-engine thing almost like a fighter and a red-hot little airplane, which was supposed to be good for people who would become B26 or P38 pilots. You sat side-by-side in a rather small space, the pilot and the instructor, and you had a door on each side like a car. The word was that if you have an accident in one and had to get out, whoever got out first on that door got his door opened, but you couldn't get the other door open. I always made damn sure I was close to where the handle was. In addition, it had a characteristic that if you should do a stall with full flaps you could not recover the stall until you got the flaps up. This was with wheels down also. It flew very well, but it was a hot landing thing and very few of us cadets ever made a really good landing with this as I recall. But fun to fly, but we didn't get too much time in that—I don't know—eight or ten hours, something like that. Most of the time was in the bamboo bomber. One thing to remember with us was that if the wind got too high, you almost had to have people run out and grab the wings of the bamboo bomber because it was hard to get it down on the ground.

Although our main field was at Frederick, we also flew out of some four auxiliary fields located around that part of Oklahoma. I remember the name of some of them were Chattanooga and Plainview and two others that I forgot the name. One of them had two runways that crossed in the middle like in a big X. One night taking off and I knew that there could be planes on the other runway—shouldn't be, but they could be. And I noticed a light that was moving that as I moved it moved. I almost chopped the throttles and almost caused an accident when I realized that what I was seeing was a light on the ground somewhere. It was stationary, but as I moved it looked like it was moving on the other runway and we were going to meet in the middle. I was flying with Crunk that night and he thought I was crazy. And I guess it scared both of us pretty good. Finally the great day came and we graduated. By then we'd had the chance to get our uniforms, and all of us had bought our new caps and immediately took the grommets out of them so the things would flop down on the side and look like we had the 50 mission crush. During our graduation review (and I've thought about this often since) white and black soldiers were mixed up together in formation. So we were pretty well integrated even then.

Long train ride back to Pensacola. By then I knew I'd been assigned to B26s, which I had not asked for. I don't think anybody asked for them because they had a pretty bad reputation at the time. We had been given a preference list, which I don't think meant much. And I had heard that some people would be selected to go to PBY training, which was a big flying boat and sent to Pensacola Naval Air Station for training. Upon graduation at Pensacola we would receive, in addition to silver wings we got as Air Force Pilots, we would also get gold Navy wings. This sounded pretty good to me because I could see myself walking the streets of Pensacola with two sets of wings. And I thought, boy, they'd be great getting girls anyway. I'd be real hero with that. As a matter of fact, it never came true for me in getting girls either. But I did run into some Navy people many years later at a museum in San Diego. And when I brought that up they said, "Were you one of those guys? We hated you people. You came in there for few months and got gold wings from us."

Having graduated from flight school and being turned out as a brand new gold bar second banana, 2nd Lt., wings, and that type thing, I did go home and spend, I think, about a ten-day leave there before I reported to Lake Charles, Louisiana for transition training. I was to be assigned to a crew there as a copilot.

B26 /CREW TRAINING

With the new shiny gold bars of a 2nd Lieutenant, I got ten days or two weeks leave and went home to Pensacola. To get there from Frederick, Oklahoma you had to first give a dollar to the first GI that saluted you, and then myself and some other guys pitched in $10 a piece to get a fellow that had a car to drive us down to Wichita Falls, Texas where we could get on a train. I think we sat up on the train all the way back. There were no berths. But I was happy to see a pine tree once I got away from prairie country around Oklahoma.

Although I had been gone a year-and-a-half, when I got home Pensacola itself hadn't changed too much. There were many changes in that there were not many boys that I knew still around, unless they just happened to be on leave. (In World War II everyone that could see daylight and hear thunder was in the service.) Still some of the old girl friends around and got out with them a couple of times, which was nice, but I was different and so were they. I felt older and they seemed younger.

My orders were for Barksdale Field at Shreveport, Louisiana for B26 training. This was not on my list of requests, as I recall, but although I didn't know it at the time—I know now—we were really being sent where somebody wanted us and where the need was. I think I'd put down P38s and PBYs, and maybe B17s or B25s, but B26 is what I got. This was not exactly something most of us chose at that time because the B26 had a pretty bad reputation. In fact, it was called various names because of the accident rate that it had. Among the names it was called included the Baltimore Whore, The Flying Prostitute, No Visible Means of Support (meaning very short wings). Some people had derided it and said it ought to have handles on the side like a casket since it killed so many in training at that time.

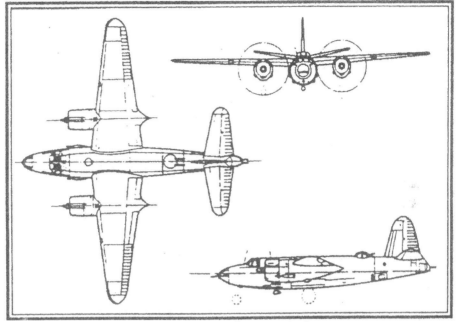

Martin B26 (Marauder)

Whatever, I was going to Barksdale Field for training as a co-pilot on a B26 crew. We stayed around Barksdale for a couple of weeks, which wasn't bad, doing mainly nothing except killing time in the Officer's Club, and downtown reconnoitering looking for girls. My good friend Tom McNamara also a B26-to-be copilot and I had one embarrassing event in the officer's club. Noon one day and he and I were in there trying to figure what to do for entertainment next. He kept leaning forward in his chair, a modernistic curved metal device, when it slipped out from under him and sailed about 10 feet across the shiny 0 Club floor. He lay flat on his back with nothing less than Colonels watching. (It seemed.) I just left. Didn't bother to help him up. Acted as though I didn't know him. Chagrin all around.

I was, however, required to become qualified with the 45 automatic while I was there. This required a truck ride out to a hot and dusty firing range. Repeatedly, as I couldn't hit diddly with that thing. After three or four days the Range Sergeant asked "Want to come back tomorrow Lieutenant?" No, I said, and with that he took my target, poked holes in it with a pencil, signed it and said "you're qualified, don't come back."

And then I was put on a train and sent ·down to Lake Charles, Louisiana to the Lake Charles Army Air Force Base. I arrived at night and didn't know anybody. I went into this barracks, which was sort of somber because it was dark. I picked out a bunk. It had happened that there'd been a crash right before I got there, so there was a lot of low talk about that. Apparently the fellow had flown so low that when he started to pull up, the tail drug and killed all of them. This was something you never really got used to.

The barracks were crowded. There were a few of the "dirt road sport" types had hung ladies' underwear up by their bunks. I assumed they were advertising for something—probably blow-hard types. I did realize, however, that maybe I'd led a sheltered life after seeing some of this. Shortly after arrival I met the crew that I was to join. A fellow by the name of Duane (Dewey) Borst from Wisconsin, who was about 23 or 24. He had been through B26 transition and was our pilot. When you finished flying school some of us were sent for crew training and others were sent through transition where they took a couple of months to specialize in particular type of airplane. That had happened to Borst. (I don't recall any of our class being sent to transition.) He had been through B26 transition, and therefore he was the pilot and I was the copilot. I was the youngest, I think, at the age of 20 as the copilot. We had a flight engineer, David Foil from Arizona (although originally from Louisiana), and David was probably 22 or 23. We had a radio operator named Jack Pappas, a Greek boy from Michigan, and he was about 26. Our bombardier, Max Kiel, was from Milwaukee. He was 26 or 27. We had a tail gunner by the name of Jack Edwards who I think was about 21 or 22. Edwards was one of the fellows that was quick to tell us that although allegedly everybody in the air crew were all volunteers, he wasn't

—he was just put into it whether he wanted aircrew or not. He didn't. Actually, that was the way Army worked and you sort of got used to it because that's the way it was.

Fortunately, David Foil had had some training at the Curtis Wright Institute before he ever came into the Army. As our flight engineer he was probably as capable as anybody on the plane. Pappas had been through radio school and was a radio operator, which turned out to be too bad because in combat we didn't carry those radios, although we did use them in the states. Edwards, of course, was tail gunner. Edwards, Foil, and Pappas had all been through gunnery training and I believe were Sergeants.

Although we had met up as a crew, we did not immediately start flying together. Initially we flew with more experienced crews or B26 instructors. It was a big jump to go from an AT17, which weighed about 5,000 or 6,000 lbs. and had two 245-hp engines to a B26, which had an unloaded weight of 32,000 lbs. and a max gross of 38,500. Instead of two 245-hp engines, we had two 2,000-hp engines, each swinging a four-bladed prop of 13-ft diameter. A real change. Sort of like sitting on the front porch driving the house. The B26 had sort of a speckled history. It was an airplane that was urgently needed, and went right from design straight into production with little testing or pilot readiness. Consequently, a lot of people really weren't ready for it. A lot of those people who came in as medium bomber pilots had probably been flying old Douglas B18s and B23s, which were sort of one jump from that bamboo bomber I trained in. Sort of slow and easy. The B26 had probably the highest wing loading of any aircraft in the Army at that time. As such, it had a very high landing speed with an approach speed of 150 mph. it would cruise on up to 250 or 260, but we usually flew around 210, which was fast enough. The airplane was redlined at 350, although I have heard of some going faster. I was in one at 350 myself one time.

It had so many accidents at first that it was being reviewed for cancellation, although they were already making them. It had such a bad accident rate that people were scared of them and didn't want to fly them. And it kept that reputation throughout its history. Mention that you flew B26s and everyone rolled their eyes. But the airplane, once you could fly it, if you could fly it, was quite a vehicle. It had very low loss rates in combat and would take tremendous battle damage. As long as the big keel, which ran down the middle to the bottom of the airplane, held together, you were together. I mentioned the people being scared of it until Jimmy Doolittle of Tokyo fame came down from somewhere—I don't know where—and demonstrated how to fly it. Flew it back and forth on one engine, including a single engine landing. That changed things a little bit. After they began to train people in how to fly it they improved and the accident rate improved. Somewhat.

However, the 322nd Group to which I was later assigned had borne the brunt of this original B26 training and indoctrination. They had trained in Tampa Florida and had had enough accidents that they used to refer to this training as "One a day in Tampa Bay." This was about how many fell in the bay while they were training there. The B26 had an ominous single engine characteristic. If single engine happened on takeoff you were going to roll on your back and crash. That is if you couldn't get the engines shut down and crash land straight ahead. The PIF (Pilot's Information File) had a statement that in the event of engine loss on takeoff, "discontinue flight." That was sort of a joke because you were damn well going to discontinue it in one way or another.

The aircraft originally had only a 65 ft wing span, with a high wing loading. Later they added 6 feet making it a 71-ft wing span to lower wing loading. Unfortunately they then added weight, with an added HP rating for each engine from 1850 HP to 2000 HP. Still high wing loading. Late in the war the G model was introduced. Without anyone knowing the G model had an increased angle of incidence; i.e. the wing angle of attack (tilt) was increased 3 1/2 degrees. This caused it to lift sooner. This was hair raising if you were expecting lift at 130 or so and it wanted to lift as slow as 100 or 110. Control of the Curtis Electric propellers was also a challenge to learn. The copilot had to get very good at this. Because the prop speed, the settings for takeoff were

51 inches of manifold pressure at 2,700 rpm on the propellers. As you applied power, prop pitch control was automatic on the Curtis Electric. However, the Curtis Electric props were known to run away sometimes exceeding desired RPMs and sometimes not speed up enough. For manual control in this emergency during takeoff there was a threeposition manual control switch for each engine. With the switch forward, it was in automatic. However, if it ran away, you were to pull it out of automatic and switch it over to slow the thing down, which should bring the rpm down below or to 2,700. Or if it wasn't going fast enough, then you had to go the other way to raise the rpm. I had to use that only occasionally. There was one other thing that you could do if it was really running away and you could not bring it down manually. That was the· feather switch to feather that engine. Feathering meant to turn the blades directly parallel to the wind flow so that it would not spin and cause drag due to propeller "wind milling." That feather switch could feather that engine in 8 seconds. So it behooved one to only barely just bump it to slow the propeller down. On takeoff this was critical.

Another thing in the cockpit was that the flap lever and the wheels actuator to pull up the wheels were side-by-side. They had a little guard on the wheels, but it was easy to make a mistake and pull the flaps up. If you did, the airplane settled back down and wouldn't fly because you needed the flaps set at about 30 (I think) degrees for lift in order to take off. The pilot always when flying with a strange or inexperienced copilot had one eye looking ahead and the other eye on the right watching the copilot's hand. And many a copilot had his hand knocked down when it looked like he was going to grab the wrong lever. Because if he did pull that—if you pull the wheels up too soon and it wasn't quite flying, it would settle, and if you were lucky it might keep going, and if not you were going to set right in on your belly. If you pulled the flaps up, it wasn't going to fly at all—there wouldn't be enough lift. We did have one fellow overseas by the name of Carmody I remember who pulled up too soon like that—pulled the wheels out from under it—and the thing settled and ticked his props. He did fly, but he barely managed to get back. It was a joke at the time, but it could have been very serious. And he was an experienced pilot.

We must have had some kind of checklist, but I frankly don't remember it. I knew that in training we had a checklist called "Cigarette" where you went through Controls, Instrument, Gas, Aileron, Rudder, Elevator, Trim, Tabs, and Elevation (for the field). But I'm sure it was more sophisticated than that on the B26. I do recall that people have asked on occasion, "You think you could still fly the thing?" I think I could if I could get the damn thing started, but it was complex. It was sort of a two-man operation when you were doing that.

In combat there were two schools of thought on how to take off. One was that you ran the airplane as fast as it would go on a 5,000-ft runway, about 150 mph. Others would pull it off and let it hang on the props as soon as it would lift. Because with those great big (swinging 13 foot diameter} four-bladed props it would sort of hang there. In that situation if one engine so much as hiccupped, you were a goner. I was a great believer in take off runs in the 150 range. Ordinarily the copilot would trade off with the pilot during flight with the pilot usually making takeoffs and landings. However, wanting to know more about this before we went overseas, I had one friend by the name of Howard Gates, a pilot from Alexandria, Louisiana (I still communicate with him at Christmas). One Sunday afternoon I managed to get some left seat pilot time with him in the right seat as instructor. Made takeoffs and landings in the daytime, and several night landings. Confidence building in the extreme. As an aside, one of my good friends, Earl Rookey, was sent in to our Group in France straight out of advanced flight training never having seen a B26. The story was that the bombardier had to show him how to get in the airplane. He later, after the war, flew several times with me as my copilot. By then he was quite proficient.

I well remember my initial B26 indoctrination flight from a big macho-type instructor in Lake Charles. He was a 1st Lieutenant on testosterone drip. I remember I flew as copilot with him and he had a cigar in his mouth. for which he was known. He also kept the left side window open. And the first time—I didn't know you could do it—but in the air you can spit and it would be sucked right out the window. That was his big haw-haw trick, spitting his tobacco juice out the window. The two 2,000-hp engines, on takeoff, literally pushed you back in your seat with the acceleration. It was something you had not felt before in flying. Needless to say it was a far cry from the AT 17 Bamboo Bomber. This particular instructor pilot showed how he could trim the airplane up for hands-off on the final approach, spit out the window, almost take his hands off the wheel, put full flaps on, and just use the rudder to kick back and forth to level the wings up. Actually, you were not supposed to use ailerons on the final to be sure you didn't stall the wing out.

One of the stories was that the airplane could come over the end of a 5,000-ft runway at 1000-foot elevation, chop the throttles drop full flaps and the thing would come down like an elevator and still make the runway all right. Not sure this is true, but it seemed that way because it did have a rapid rate of descent. You spent most of your time spinning the elevator control tab wheel to keep the nose up because you could not hold the nose up if you did not do that.

I might have mentioned that this hotshot instructor there in Lake Charles did eventually join our Squadron in France much later—quite late in the war—as a copilot. Also, he didn't have quite the bravado once he was flying combat. It seemed to chill him a little bit.

In Lake Charles when we did start flying together, Borst and I and the others, we became a team and a good. one. As I mentioned, Foil, our flight engineer, was very capable. That airplane had a fuel transfer requirement where it had a fuel transfer panel and a bunch of valves for fuel transfer. (It was necessary to transfer fuel between tanks on longer flights.) I have to admit I never had a clue as to what he was doing. Not until many years later while reviewing a B26 Pilot's Handbook—I was a graduate engineer then—did I understand exactly what he was doing. Of course at the time I was 20 years old and wasn't too sure of what the hell I was doing some of the time anyway.

But as time went on, we did a fair amount of transition flying together and flew at night, flew formation, did some night formations, which I thoroughly despised because I couldn't see that well it seemed to me. The B26 had little, tiny, blue lights on top of it and as you flew you were supposed to fly formation on those lights, which seemed like sure suicide to me. But nevertheless we lived through it. Night formation, as I say, was one of my less favorite challenges. On the coast in Louisiana, weather was also a problem. We could be up in all kinds of weather and occasionally ground fog would come in and they would announce that flying was called off. Everybody was to come in. I don't know how many airplanes we had there—it seemed like a million, but probably 30 or 40—but everybody trying to get back into the landing pattern with fog coming in was pretty exciting.

Low level flying was forbidden except for training purposes and we did have one cross-country low level flight. For that I did not fly with the regular crew, but flew with another bunch that I did not know. This pilot was a true wild man, and although I believe we were briefed to be at 500 ft, he was down low enough to almost knock the farm houses down. I remember watching little kids run, scared to death, and cows and horses rear up when we went over them as we were right down on the deck. I don't know whatever became of this fellow, as he probably killed himself somewhere because he seemed hell-bent on trying that anyway. We also flew some practice bombing missions where we'd take blue practice bombs up to a bombing range called Kisatchie (K3) in northern Louisiana. The crew on the ground in manning this bombing range was supposed to be called in order to get approval to bomb. We soon learned that this was a black crew up there who I'm not sure knew what they were doing, but they weren't paying much attention to radio. It was almost always necessary to call, and call, and call with no answer, and finally we would drop a few bombs, which had a smoke charge them. And with that the radio came alive—"What y'all doing, what y'all doing?" Woke them up anyway.

We did fly in some pretty crummy weather, not through thunderstorms but they were around and you could see these big cumulonimbus clouds lighting up at night when you were flying in between. Pretty light displays but also pretty dangerous. We did have instruction on how to fly through thunderstorms— if you had to penetrate one. Those who were sent the southern route to Europe where they flew across the south Atlantic might have had use for it. We did not thankfully, as we went the northern route through Greenland. I remember an instructor telling us that if caught in a situation where you would have to fly through a thunderstorm how to proceed. The idea was to take off your headsets because the noise would be terrible from the thunder and lighting. If you had a blind flying hood, put it up because it was also very terrifying to see the water just pouring in across the windshield. Slow the airplane down to 150 mph, which is slow for that airplane, and then concentrate only on flying level. Pay no attention to the altitude because you were going to rise and fall 5,000 feet in these updrafts and downdrafts. This would surely have been a terrifying experience. Luckily we never had to do that. But we were prepared to do that if need be.

One of the saddest things that happened was one of the accidents we had where the entire crew was killed, and it happened in the morning, and we knew it. We soon found that one of the fellows was a boy by the name of Arlie Kuehn, whom I had known as a cadet in Illinois. I remember because he was one of the fellows that slipped on some ice, fell and busted his mouth up. I can still see the guy with his mouth busted up like he'd been in a bad fist fight. He was now a Bombardier. The entire crew was killed. His wife had come down to visit him, and we knew that she was waiting in the officer's club to have dinner with him. No one had the guts to go over and tell her that they were all dead. Finally we found the chaplain and got him to go over and tell her. A sad experience. Of course as these experiences grew I suppose it hardened us.

We were flying a number of cross-country flights. Some of

those turned out to be somewhat more than interesting. Once we had to make an emergency landing in Little Rock, Arkansas because all the lights had gone out on the airplane. I can remember Dewey, the pilot, flying with me holding the flashlight on the airspeed indicator making a landing. When we got on the ground— he made the landing all right and we could see the runway lights— but as we started to turn off the first turn off place, there sat a fire truck that had been called out on the field. Except that the stupid guy didn't have his lights on. We came within an inch of just putting these big four-bladed props right through that fire engine. On another flight, which turned out to be sort of funny, we went to Oklahoma City, and when we got there we got instructions as to where we could stay. At that time there were lots of soldiers and they sent us to an old rooming house. It was run by an old lady who as soldiers came in—officers or whatever—you got assigned a bed. The next morning—and we never let Pappas, the radio operator live this down—Pappas woke up and in the bed with him was the old lady of about 75 years old. It seems that her practice was to keep assigning boys to beds and then she just got in the last one there was and that was Pappas. He swore he had no part of this, but we never let him forget it.

I had one very interesting dental event at Lake Charles. I had a bad wisdom tooth that had to come out. I went on sick call to the dentist. (Actually, as I said earlier, I never had to go on sick call my entire time in the Army except for dental work. Just healthy I guess.) It turned out it was of sufficient interest to the Dental Corps of the Air Force that they decided to hold a symposium on it. I had a Colonel take it out with a whole bunch of lesser-light dentists standing around watching. It didn't hurt, but I can remember him breaking the thing apart with some sort of hammer drill in my mouth, although there was no pain since I was well deadened. He took it out in pieces and then told me I could have the day off and to rinse with salty water. I had no idea where the hell I was going to find salty water in the barracks, but at least I got a day off.

Probably more than passing excitement was when we realized

there was a family of skunks underneath the barracks and everyone made sure to not alarm them or in any way to upset them. I don't know whatever became of them, but we didn't bother them and they didn't bother us.

We did see one guy come in one time making a wheels-up landing in a P40. Apparently something had gone wrong with it. We went out and watched as it slid down the runway. And by the time he stopped, the fire trucks were out there with these enormous jets of foam. They covered that airplane up with a mountain of foam. The pilot tried to beat his way out of it. He wasn't hurt. He was trying to climb out but had so much foam on him he could hardly get out of the plane. He was waving his hands to get them to stop.

The B26s we were using in Lake Charles were pretty well used up. I heard that after we left they had several accidents where they would not hold on single engine. One of my friends from cadets, Tony Gerlach, was lost when one went in the Gulf. Speaking of the Gulf we had a final cross country (try water) across the Gulf of Mexico from Lake Charles to Tampa. Uneventful but you got the feeling that you were SOL if something happened out over the ocean. I think that may have been what happened to Gerlach. No single engine capability. And we had the ocean coming up after Lake Charles. The Atlantic.

Duane R Borst	Eugene G Cowart	Wm. "Max" Kiel	David A Foil	J B Pappas	Jack D Edward
Pilot	CoPilot	Bombardier	Flt Engr	Radio operator	Tail Gunner
Ashland, WI	Pensacola, Fl	Milwaukee, Wi	Winslow, Az	Akron, Ohio	Okla City, Ok

LAKE CHARLES/ TRANSATLANTIC/ PRESTWICK

While in Lake Charles we flew with various instructor pilots from time to time. One that remains vividly in my mind was a fellow named De Fan, another Lieutenant, who had served an overseas tour and was supposed to be knowledgeable of combat conditions. I don't know what he had done overseas, but he didn't seem to know much about some of the more modern navigation devices. He flew with us one night and thought we were lost and got totally panicked. We finally convinced him that between our dead-reckoning navigation and radio compass we were in no way lost. Finally it calmed him down. But he was of no use as an instructor.

Another unpleasant event we had were the Flight Surgeons who would occasionally fly with us. A Flight Surgeon was a doctor in the Air Force. Not all of them were Flight Surgeons, but some were. They had to get four hours of flying time per month to get their flight pay, which I think was what they were really interested in. One fellow came down one night that we didn't know and wanted to fly with us. This meant that he just sat in the radio compartment for four hours and got his flight pay. On this night, however, we had terrible weather. Thunderstorms were in the area, which were quite common in the springtime. Also, ground fog was forecast to be probable later—sort of a really sticky night. And finally we were all called back in to return— flying was called off for that night. He didn't know this, but we had quite a time getting back with everyone else trying to land. We landed, and taxied up. When we stopped he said, "you only got three and a half hours." (Damned whiner.) I think he was a Captain and we couldn't tell him anything other than, well, flying got called off. He made somewhat of a scene because he then knew he was going to have to fly again another night. Wanted his four hours for flight pay.

I've mentioned weather, which was sometimes good, sometimes bad, and sometimes bad and beautiful along with it. I do remember one night when we were flying in between layers of clouds and there were thunderstorms in the area. And out in the distance you could see these things just columns of light when the lightning would flash in them. It was almost like flying in marble halls. But sort of dangerous if you flew into them.

We finally completed training at Lake Charles and were bound for overseas. We boarded a train in Lake Charles bound for Savannah, Georgia where we would pick up an airplane at Hunter Air Force Base. The train would go through Flomaton, Alabama, which is a town in south Alabama. I knew, however, when we got to Flomaton and felt the train back down—it went down towards Pensacola—I knew then we were going to go through Pensacola, my hometown. When it got into the station in Pensacola, the L&N Station—I remember it well because that's where I left from when I enlisted over a year or so before—1 got off the train and called my folks and told my mother I was passing through and leaving. Well, with that she picked up the phone and called the railroad station and asked them how long the troop train would be there. The operator told her there were no troop trains here and that there was nothing in the station. She then realized that this was a secret troop movement and that no one could say who was here and who was not. Nevertheless, my mother and father jumped in the car and came down to the station. The train was still there and I had gotten back in my bunk when the train commander came through looking for me. He stated, "Why didn't you tell me this was your hometown? Your mother and father are outside on the platform. Get out and talk to them." Which I did. One of the few people leaving overseas that did get to talk to his mother and father before he left.

We eventually got to Savannah, picked up our gear. Everybody got a 45 automatic. Of course we had no ammunition although we did have a pistol. We also got an airplane assigned to us and had to get familiar with it and box the compass, turn it around and around on the hard stand to be sure that the compass was reading right. We were then briefed on the route. We were going to go from Savannah to Dow Field, Bangor, Maine, from Bangor, Maine to Goose Bay, Labrador, from Goose Bay, Labrador to BWl (Bluie West One, just north of Cape Farewell in Greenland), from there to Keflavik, Iceland, and from Keflavik, Iceland to Prestwick, Scotland. This seems straightforward enough considering that you had a new airplane and a new crew with me being the youngest at 20 and the oldest being about 26 or 27—the pilot, Borst, having probably at that time 400 or 500 hours maybe, and I having maybe 350 hours in flight, but a bunch of boys taking off and away we went.

The first thing we did was fly directly over the Nation's capital, Washington, DC, which was a proscribed area—you're not supposed to fly over it. Nevertheless, we went over it with all six of us up in the cockpit trying to see below.

We got to Dow Field in Bangor, Maine with no problems going nonstop from Savannah to Dow. (I should mention here that we had belly tanks in the airplane for long-range, over-water travel.) I remember very well a lady in the Red Cross stationed there at Dow in Bangor asking me how I liked Maine. It was fairly warm that day as I recall, and I stated it seemed very nice. I remember the old lady looking at me and saying, "Well you wouldn't like it in the winter time. Nobody does. It's too cold."

After a few days we eventually started on the next leg to go to Goose Bay, Labrador. We were hardly up to altitude out of Bangor, Maine when both engines started alternating cutting out one after the other. Truly not good in an airplane, especially one like this with a young crew starting a transatlantic flight. We managed to get to Presque Isle, Maine, which was not far. We had to make a 360-degree turn coming down on final and landing with engine one cut out and then the other one back and forth. When this had happened, we had told Edwards, the tail gunner, to go back in the bomb bay and flip the tank/bomb switch. There was a switch on the tanks where if you flipped one way the tanks were secure in the airplane. If you should have to drop the tanks (salvo), you'd throw the switch the other way and could drop those tanks, which you could do in an emergency landing. You didn't want all that fuel in there. Nevertheless, we did get down and land. And at that time realized that Edwards had sort of got paralyzed and was standing on the keel in the bomb bay and had not thrown those switches. He was ready to jump and apparently failed to throw the switch. It would have been a real mess it we had crashed, because we would have had a hell of a bonfire.

We had the engineering people at Presque Isle Air Base look over the engine. No one could find anything wrong with it. And finally they swapped out all the plugs on it. Dewey and I (and Foil?) took it up for a test flight. Not our favorite thing to do, a little pinchy. It seemed to run all right. So all aboard and away we went on our way to Goose Bay, Labrador. We stayed in Goose Bay for a couple of days and from there we then took off over water, the Davis Straits, for "Bluie" (**military code for Greenland-- Bluie West One is now Narsarsuaq Airport**). Now, at altitude that far north it is very, very clear. You can see a long distance. And we began to see Greenland but it seemed like hours before we got to it. We immediately accused Kiel, who was supposed to be keeping up with navigation—actually we were on a radio compass— but it seemed like he'd missed our ETA as we seemed to be almost there. However, we flew for quite a while before getting there.

Greenland, from a distance, looks like something prehistoric. It's all covered in ice, real high mountains and peaks, snow everywhere. In addition, to get into BWI it was necessary to fly up a fjord to where the air base was. They gave us lectures on how to get in there. There were three ways to go in, depending on the weather. One, if you were lucky you saw a scratched off place where a radio tower was, and that meant you were at the right fjord, and you could go in with visual conditions and fly right up the fjord to the air base. The other two required that you follow a different fjord if that one was socked in, which could happen from time to time. On another one it would also lead you to the air base. The most treacherous, or perilous, was one where you had to fly down a certain fjord and at a certain point pick up into the overcast and fly over some mountains on instruments and then drop down, and if you were lucky (timed it right) you were at the air base. This was a real concern and luckily we saw it was visual when we got in and got to go directly in without a problem.

We were weathered-in in Greenland for it seemed like about a week and couldn't get out. We were in a barracks with some RAF people who were flying B25s over. Also while we were there a B24 landed and washed out its nose gear and almost came off the end of the runway down into the barracks where we were living.

However, a perilous thing that happened concerning the heavy bombers, which usually did not land in Greenland. They hit Cape Farewell at the southern tip of Greenland and turned south to the Azores. From there on to Europe or wherever they were going. One night—we could listen to it on the radio—we heard a B17 that was in trouble. He was in the overcast, apparently iced up (?) and had spun once or twice, tore off an aileron, navigator had jumped, crew knocked around, the copilot was flying as the pilot had been disabled. They were trying to get down and just couldn't make it for fear of mountains. They got up above the overcast— the nights were only about an hour long—until a Major stationed on that airfield went up in what I believe was an AT6, which is an advanced single engine trainer. He found them above the overcast and led the guys down to the field and saved the whole crew. These people were all bunged up and we knew this because the airplane when it spun had thrown them all around, some of the crew were not strapped in. We had a firsthand account of this because our Bombardier, Max Kiel, who said he never intended to get overseas anyway, and went on sick call every time we landed somewhere, had managed to get himself in the hospital with that crew. As an aside, Max could say I've taken a cold and in five minutes his nose would run and his eyes would be red and he'd be deathly ill. He went on sick leave saying maybe I'll have to stay behind everywhere we landed. Dewey always had to go to the hospital to get him out of sick bay to keep him going with us. But he did give us a report on this B17 crew. The Navigator who jumped was later written up in the EverReady flashlight battery ads because when he jumped—and Greenland only has a population of about 0.2 per square miles—he came down swinging a flashlight at an Eskimo village at the end of the runway. Talk about luck.

Night was only about an hour long, and you never knew when you went to bed when you woke up whether it was daylight or still night, because it was a very short time. The RAF people were flying B25s and made statements there was no reason to ever have to quit flying because of weather and went ahead and took off in their 25s and got out of there. I remember watching them take off because they would run the B25 up and pull back on the control yoke and the thing would rear up like a horse. I had never seen that before. This RAF attitude about weather also was disastrous in some cases as Bomber Harris, Air Marshall of the RAF, sent bomber crews up in all kinds of weather and many iced up and spun in. Once later near our base in France. RAF Bomber crews referred to him as Butcher Harris.

After about a week, we did get away ourselves. And going towards Iceland, when you took off you had to cross over the ice cap about 12000 feet high. I remember us going over it barely hanging there at about 150 mph climbing trying to get over the ice. The airplane was max gross loaded with fuel at around 38,500 lbs., which was all it would do. We literally crept over the ice. Had we had a single engine I'm not sure what would have happened as we could not have held altitude. (Thoughts of the earlier engine problems were always present.) I actually have a good idea of what would have happened. Not good.

We did get to Keflavik, Iceland and if there ever was a barren-looking god forsaken place that's it. The field at Keflavik was sort of rocky and not much to look at. We were put in a hut way out from the main part of the field and lived out there other than when we were transported in to eat. We had one fellow with us that had trained with us in Lake Charles. We called him Pop, Akers was his last name, who was about 27 years old. He also had the distinction of having gone through B25s in Advance Flight Training rather than the usual AT17-type aircraft. Some kind of experimental training program. On the night before we left Lake Charles we went down to the Chapel and the Chaplain gave a good bye and god bless sermon. Akers had a suitcase full of whiskey and was on the front row and put the clinking bunch of bottles underneath his seat. When we got to Iceland, where apparently liquor was unavailable, one of the field's Crew chiefs saw that he had whiskey and tried to buy some from him. Akers refused to sell him any and the Crew Chief then says, "In that case I'm gonna put the Iceland curse on you and that means you'll never get home." Sobering thought. I'd have given it to him. Don't know if Akers ever made it back.

We stayed there several days and I was not sad to leave it because it was truly a barren, destitute looking place. Only funny thing I remember was that at that time there was a comic strip about aviators in the newspapers, "Terry and the Pirates." Some of the aviators in the comic strip had campaign-type hats—the old-time, flat brimmed things that were earlier used in the Army. They had some of these hats for sale in the PX there, but they were forbidden to sell them to any air crew because the guys would have bought one and put there headsets over it and wrapped it around their head to show off. Just like "Terry and the Pirates."

Up to this point my recollection is that we had fuel to get to the place we were going and return if need be. (Bomb Bay tanks.) However, going from Iceland to Scotland, you had a point of no return, no turning back, you had to go on. No turning back because you didn't have enough fuel to get back. Somewhere not too far out of Scotland we ran into some just terrible-looking weather. Thick, clouds with overcast all around, yellowish-looking, clouds like big yellow puff balls all over the place, also pretty cold. The airplane started doing some odd vibration or acting up at that time. Nothing for it then but to keep on going, making land over Stornaway on the Isle of Lewis in the Hebrides, finally landing in Prestwick, Scotland. Needless to say we were relieved (there's an understatement) when we did pick up Stornaway, flying in over it and over a place called the Island of Mull.

Now this is big time. We're at a big RAF base with all kinds of people there in all kinds of airplanes. I'm a 20-year-old Pilot in the US Army Air Corps. I'm away to the Officer's Club there (a mature? 20-year-old,). Not being very bright anyway I went in and ordered a Scotch and Soda. Now I had never drunk Scotch and Soda in my life, but it seemed like the thing to do since I was the aforementioned US Lieutenant and a pilot in an RAF officers club. Just like the movies. Worst tasting stuff I've ever had in my life. I finally managed to get it down. In later life while I prefer Scotch, I still don't drink it with soda. I'm not sure whether I poured this in a potted plant or not, but I managed to get rid of it. Also, they didn't believe in ice as I recall, and this really was a dose. I learned a little bit from that however.

After we stayed there a very short time we took the airplane and delivered it to a Depot in Burtonwood, England, in the Blackpool or Liverpool area. We were through with it. As it turned out that airplane showed up in our Group later and was forever being worked on. It seemed to have some kind of a problem in the fuel lines. Lucky us, we got over the ocean with it, but other than the vibration towards the end had no further problems with it.

I remember in Burtonwood for the first time really starting to eat British. (The English are so known for their cuisine.) Some gray, brown-looking bread, which tasted like hell, and sink hole coffee. Also, instead of a mattress, they gave us three square donut-looking things for a mattress to sleep on and a horse blanket, which was a gray woolen thing that would have been good for sandpaper. Another memory is that the first major air base we landed in—maybe it was Prestwick or maybe down at Burtonwood—we got in too late for the regular mess line and were told we could go over and eat in this rather large dining hall. Got in there and was sitting down when I saw this fellow coming from the distance. I could tell he was a Lt. Colonel, wings of a flying officer, and walking straight towards me. I immediately tried to think of someone I might know. (Lots of Pensacola boys in the Army Air Corps). I thought, how lucky, somebody I know and he's a Colonel. (Ever the eternal optimist.) He walked right up to me, put his hand on my flight jacket, grabbed the epaulet, and said, "Flight jackets—keep them out of the mess hall," and walked off. At that time, our people in England were trying to act like the RAF. Great welcome to England and the war.

IRELAND

Stayed in Burtonwood, England for several days after we delivered our airplane to the depot there. Our crew and a bunch of others were loaded into a C47 and flown across the Irish Channel to Northern Ireland. We landed at a remote landing strip miles from nowhere in a driving rain. No one there to greet us, meet us, or what have you. The C47 pilots said, "Well, My job was to put you here. And here you are and we're leaving." So we stood around in the rain for awhile, soaking wet, and wondering what the hell now. In time, trucks came up and picked us up and took us back to a base near Toomebridge, Northern Ireland for more training. We were set up in Nissan huts. I forget how many were in the hut, but I do remember one other crew that was in there with a pilot I believe named Linkous. One of the funny things was that in flying over they'd let their flight engineer come up and sit in the left seat and "drive" when it was long, straight flights going across the ocean, no weather or anything. They said flying straight and level was too dull, so they let him do it. And it made him feel like he was flying the ocean. If I remember right, this crew did not make it through the war.

Another good friend of ours was a fellow by the name of Ruben Corbin. My recollection of him is because my has married a fellow who is the spitting image of him—looks exact1y like him. In fact, its uncanny. Ruben was also killed. He was not in our group, but in another one.

We received numerous lectures on aircraft recognition while training in Ireland. I remember being told that we were to be very careful in talking to the Irish and never getting into political arguments. The IRA was quite active in the area at that time. In

Belfast the police would still patrol at night with rifles. The word was that we might think we were having a political discussion and they were planning to knock you in the head if they disagreed with you. Apparently there was one constable, an Irish policeman, there that arrested some bigwig in the IRA and the British had to get him out of Ireland and send him to India to get away. So the troubles in Ireland are not new—they've been going on a long time.

I remember all of us getting in a rubber raft and practicing as though we had ditched in the channel, which did happen quite often. Must have been a scene, all of us sitting in that silly raft in a small lake there, **Lough Neagh**.

We also all bought bicycles. The way to get around on that base was walk or get a bike. There was an old man by the name of Diamond who sold second hand bikes. Mr. Diamond, who it turned out had been in the States for some time until he was deported for bootlegging. He had the bicycle deal there and we all bought bicycles from him. Some did get seriously hurt trying to ride a bicycle across some small bridge. When we were getting ready to be shipped out, we wanted to sell those bicycles back to Mr. Diamond, and of course he was exacting his pound of flesh and wasn't going to give us anything for them. So being young and ignorant, we decided, well, we'll just ship them on to us in England. They were all left in a warehouse when we left and paid to have them shipped to us. Of course you had to be pretty young and dumb to understand that there was a war going on and nobody was going to ship any bicycles anywhere. Finally Mr. Diamond, I understand, broke into the warehouse and stole all the bicycles back. That was the end of our bicycle riding.

We did a fair amount of flying at that time, supposedly to be broken in as to how it would be in flying with a Bomb Group. We flew all over Northern Ireland and I can remember going over Enniskillen, and also the Giant's Causeway up in the northern tip of Ireland, which has these giant basaltic stones or rocks all in squares or octagon shapes. We were told to never fly over the Republic of Ireland, which bordered us there. One crew that did, a fellow by the name of Oscar Jones, who was in our group in England and France had the ill fortune to make a forced landing in Ireland. He was coming in after flying the Southern route from Marrakech (?) and should have been interned. However, the Irish kept the airplane, but packed him and the crew up in a truck and put them over the border. I believe Jones was Flight Officer, a bastard rank that was inflicted on some at the end of flight training. or who had started as flying Sergeant pilots. These people were not commissioned officers and if captured by the Germans were put in labor battalions like enlisted men. He and his crew should have been interned. Failure to be interned and kept out of the war made you eligible for execution by the Germans if you were captured. I believe it was here that we also got to fly in one of the original old short-wing B26s. There were very few of them still in operation at that time. A nice flying airplane once it got in the air, but it did make you wonder whether it was going to get in the air. I also remember riding in one that had no controls on the copilot's side, only some sort of round navigational device sticking up out of the floor—very uncomfortable to ride in it, nothing much you could do besides look out the window.

We also got lectures on escape and evasion, how to false count, what we could expect in a German Prison Camp. They told us— and whether this was true or not—that they would know when we went down if we stayed in a prison camp more than three weeks. That meant that we were collaborating. Don't know if that was true or not. But the Germans did first put you in a pretty nice place and were pretty buddy-buddy with you to try and get something out of you. And if you didn't talk, kept clammed up, only name, rank, and serial number, in a very short time you went on to one of the regular Stalags that they had scattered across Europe.

We also had our picture taken in rough-looking farmer-type civilian clothes, hair mussed up, and were given that picture. The idea was that the underground in occupied Europe had a difficult times taking pictures of people. The idea was that if we had that picture they could forge our identity papers for us and use that to escape. A great deal of instruction was given on escape and evasion, and, as I say, how to false count, which was to confuse the Germans. The idea was that the Germans were quite meticulous in their record keeping and that could drive them crazy. I have since heard from some people in the prison camps that there was not much funny stuff going on. But I recommend the account of a remarkable escape by a fellow from our Group, now a Federal Judge, the Honorable Anthony A. Alaimo, who was shot down on his first or second mission. He was born in Italy, but was an American citizen. He could speak Italian and did escape although it took him two years. I have heard him speak and I have a copy of his account, which is quite interesting. [It is included in *Story of the 450th Bomb Squadron, Ninth Airforce* [sic], compiled and edited by Gene Bluhm (G. Mills, 1997). See also Vincent Coppola, *The Sicilian Judge: Anthony Alaimo, an American Hero* (Macon, GA: Mercer University Press, 2009). Alaimo died, age 89, in 2009. —Ed.]

On completion of training, which lasted several weeks, we were taken down to Belfast and put on a small coastal freighter. It had an all-Malay-looking oriental crew and nondescript-looking ship's officers. We went across the Irish Channel at night. Luckily there were no submarines. The men's latrine—and I'm sure there was no lady's room on there—had six commodes, all with no seat on them. Sort of a prison-type set up. Luckily we were only on the ship overnight. Besides that they had rather odd food, and that was about it.

On landing in Liverpool we boarded a train for London. We got into London about dawn, and I remember lying down on the concrete floor of Liverpool Station in my class A uniform and going sound asleep, along with thousands of other soldiers of various nationalities, all lying around in there. From there we went from London to a place called Great Saling (later Andrews Field), which was near Chelmsford in what the English call the Wash. Believe this was out in Essex, where it was almost wall-to-wall airfields.

A stylized reproduction of the 450th Bomb Squadron's
fighting moose insignia, one of 1200 or so designed
for Allied forces by the Disney studios

322ND ENGLAND

After enlisting in November of 1942, going through the various flight schools and training, operational training of the B26 in Lake Charles, flying the ocean, Operational training in North Ireland we finally got to the war in England in the early Fall of 44. Although D-Day had occurred before in early June, 1944, the battle for Europe was in full fling. As Allies were trying to cross occupied Europe and invade Germany, the Germans in no way let up. Some of the great battles of the war in Europe were about to occur.

We were assigned to the 450th Bomb Squadron of the 322nd Bomb Group (Medium) of the 9th Air Force. Based in Great Saling in England in Essex, this was the oldest B26 group in Northern Europe. The B26 had been used for a short while in the Pacific, after which it was taken out of service there as not being suitable for that operation. It was used in North Africa and Italy earlier in the 12th Air Force. However, the 322nd was the first of some eight B26 groups that were out of England originally, first starting in the 8th Air Force and then being transferred into the 9th Air Force where I flew. Later all 8 were moved over on the continent as the allies advanced. We were, of course, a replacement crew moving into an operational outfit that had been flying for quite a while. Many of the hands in it were old timers who had flown some 40 missions, the original tour for a medium, been given leave, gone home and some had then come back to continue on towards 65 missions. At this time a tour for the heavies, B24 and B17s, was 35 missions. Heavy bombers during 43 flying out of England had a tour of 25 missions without fighter escort. They had a statistical chance of one in three of living to complete a tour. The 322nd group had had a particularly difficult entry into the war when in early 1943 they attempted low-level missions. Originally the B26 was to be operational at low-level—and attempted this flying into Holland with 12 airplanes. They bombed a power station in Holland and came home without a loss. It was then found that the bombs had not gone off, not fused properly, and the Group had to go back. They then went back to bomb again with 11 airplanes and on the way one had engine trouble and pulled up. It was thought that this alerted the German radar because when they got there a hot reception resulted in the horrific loss of all airplanes. This, the Group's introduction to combat, was the mission on which Lt Alaimo, a copilot, was shot down. He was the only survivor of his crew.

What follows is historian Trevor Allen's account of this mission (as posted on B26.com).

17th May 1943 Mission Target Ijmuiden
322 BG /450 & 452 SQ Scheduled: 11 B26's

Aborted: 41-18058 ER-S Capt. R D Stephens 450BS

Point of Entry:
Forced south of intended point of entry after being fired on by flak from German coastal convoy and flew over heavily defended Rozenburg island. Continued to target and subsequent fate. As the first flight flew over the sand dunes a hail of 20mm flak hit the lead B26 piloted by Lt. Col. Robert W Stillman, killing Lt. Resweber, the copilot. The plane snap rolled and crashed. Three severely injured crewmen were dragged from the wreckage by the Germans. A mile or two to the south the following flight also encountered heavy flak on landfall in. Lt. Garrambone, leading the second element, could not maintain control after being hit and crashed into the Maas River, he and three of his crew survived. The surviving B26's headed between Delft and Rotterdam with Capt. Converse leading the first flight. Near Bodegraven, while carrying out violent evasive action, Converse collided with Lt. Wolfe who was leading the second element. Both

B26's crashed in flames with only two survivors. Lt. Wurst's aircraft, severely damaged by debris from the two colliding aircraft, belly landed his unmanageable B26 into a field at Meije. All escaped although Sgt. Heski lost a foot. Now only the third element of the leading flight remained. Lt. F.H. Matthew, leading Lt. E.R. Norton and apparently lost, turned to join Lt. Col. Purinton's flight, but Purinton too had no idea where he was. Forty-five miles into Holland he decided to turn for home and his navigator, Lt. Jefferis, gave him a course of 2700. Almost simultaneously Jefferis reported that he had sighted the target. Bombs were dropped on what they thought were the Haarlem works, but it was in fact a gas holder in the suburbs of Amsterdam. Having climbed to bombing altitude several Marauders failed to reduce height as they headed for the coast. Unknown to the crews they were heading directly towards Ijmuiden and its murderous flak barrage. Purinton's bomber was hit, but he managed to ditch offshore near a fishing boat, manned by Germans. Jefferis was killed in the crash, but the rest of the crew were rescued to become prisoners of war. The Ijmuiden flak also claimed the bombers of Lt. Jones and Lt. Norton. One, with an engine on fire, turned back and crashed into the sea near Castricum, the other went into the sea a few miles west of Ijmuiden. Tail gunner Longworth was the only survivor from Norton's B26 and Lt. Alaimo from Jones's. Lt. Matthews and Capt. Crane had survived the Ijmuiden flak, and several miles apart headed for England. At 12.18hrs Capt. Crane was shot down into the sea by Feldwebel Niederreichholz of II/JG1 and at 12.30hrs Lt. Matthews was shot down into the sea by Ober-Feldwebel Winkler of 4/JG1. The only survivors of these two actions were S/Sgt. George W Williams and S/Sgt. Jesse H Lewis from Capt. Crane's B26. They were picked up from their rubber dinghy on 22 May 1943 by a Royal Navy vessel.

Times:
11.51 hrs Stillman   Flak, crashed

11.52	Garrambone	Flak, crashed into Maas River
11.58	Converse	Mid air collision, crashed
11.58	Wolfe	Mid air collision, crashed
11.58	Wurst	Hit by debris from mid air collision, crashed
12.12	Purinton	Flak, ditched at sea
12.13	Jones	Flak, crashed at sea
12.13	Norton	Flak, crashed at sea
12.18	Crane	Shot into sea by enemy fighters
12.30	Matthew	Shot into sea by enemy fighters

In summary: of the 10 airplanes that attacked with a complement of 60 airmen, casualties were as follows:

KIA-22

POW-24 (one committed suicide as a POW)

MIA-11 (presumed dead in channel)

Repatriated-1 (flail arm injury, Germans returned as unfit for further service)

Returned-2 (rescued by British in Channel).

The second mission of the war was a disaster. This mentally marked our Group and B26 outfits in general. B26 tactics were then reviewed and changed to mid level bombing altitudes. Probably why I was able to survive when later assigned to the 322nd. (Time and propinquity favored me.) There was one exception however. Namely our Group's raid of February 22nd, 1945. I was there. Sometimes you have to go and pay the price.

This caused great consternation with a lot of review as to what the B26 could do. It became apparent that to attempt low-level work against someone like the German Army with good automatic weapons was disastrous. They then fell back, retrained and began to bomb from 11,500 altitude, occasionally lower, occasionally higher, with excellent loss results.

Fortunately (for me) I was not yet in England for that early mission into Holland. But was in one later low-level mission on February 22nd, 1945 mentioned earlier and described later.

Our earliest activity after joining the 322nd in England occurred during the attack across the Rhine (made famous by the movie *A Bridge Too Far*). Airborne troops were passing over our field at Great Saling in gliders. Some of the gliders would break loose over our field and we had to take the British soldiers back to their base in Oxford. We had the radio room full of about six British commandos (some kind of "bad-looking dudes"). They were all in camouflage, paint on their face, garroting wire (wire with two handles for strangling someone), heavy weapons all over them and most of them young. One of the fellows was older though, a man in his forties and stated with a heavy British accent, "All these kids can't wait to get there. As for me I have been fighting in North Africa for three years and I don't give a f—k if I never get there!" With these fellows in the radio room, all of them looking right on edge, I was afraid somebody would make a sudden move and they might shoot somebody. We got them back to Oxford and left them there to fight another day.

The medium bomber bombing element was a six-ship javelin formation, which was standard for a Flight. Look at your hand with the palm down and your three middle fingers. That was the first three airplanes in a flight. Right underneath them and immediately lower and behind them, another three airplanes would follow the second three. This was a six-ship Flight, and position number one was the lead, number two I believe was on the right, number three on the left. And then right underneath the lead airplane and slightly behind him was number 4 (usually the deputy lead), and on his right was number 5, and on his left was number six. So you had a compact formation of six airplanes, the bombing element. There were usually two "boxes" of three flights each, giving 18 airplanes in a box. The group had two boxes resulting in 36 aircraft. The Bomb Group, outbound, was in a long straight climb at approximately 180 lAS (Indicated Air Speed). Once over the bomb line (enemy territory): evasive action was begun. This could entail twisting and turning, 20 degrees left, 30 right, 15 left, 10 left and so on. Altitude was constant. Bombing was by 6 ship flight, with a Bombardier and bombsight in the flight leader's airplane (also available in No.4 if leader was shot down) with all airplanes dropping bombs when the leader dropped. However, if it was an instrument flight whereby the weather was too bad (overcast, no visibility) you had to fly a G-mission, where there was one Pathfinder airplane (from a special pathfinder squadron) out front using G techniques featuring a radio beam for target location. Then the entire group bombed as one. Otherwise, when you went in with the 18, one box of 18 airplanes first, with three flights of six each. As you approach the target the lead flight in the group homes in on the target, until the IP, is reached. At that point the bombardier in the flight's lead airplane basically takes control of the aircraft by operating the Norden bombsight which controls the PDI (Pilot's Direction Indicator), i.e. the direction guiding the pilot to the target. At this time, with the doors open and flying straight and level, aircraft in a "dirty" condition. You are pretty much a sitting duck if they get on you with flak. And usually they could. An excellent bomb run might take a minute of straight and level but often it was longer, much longer. In a worse case, something goes wrong (Bombardier can't locate or track target) and your Flight needs to take a second run. Agony. And once in a while another. The second two flights, one left and one right, one slightly higher and one slightly lower than the lead flight pulled off to the left and right respectively so that you came in from the aforementioned slightly different angle, hopefully timed such that the German flak could not track each flight. The idea being that they might get on the first one but the second one would be on them before they could switch over and start firing at them. This was the idea anyway, I'm not sure it always worked too well. Each flight set up to bomb one after the other with each flight homing on the target. The idea was that if you went in at the right rate, the Germans could not track all of the box's three flights. After that the next box would come in like that. Sadly, sometimes the flights failed to achieve the right spacing. Then they could pick you up and track each flight all the way in. You could do evasive action before you got the IP with about a second of safety for every 1000 foot of altitude with a German 88; i.e. The Flight leader should take evasive turns about every 10 seconds.

From IP to target it was straight and level to the target. You sit there and take it. We called it cutting button holes in the seat. Another factor was bomb drop interval. or spacing. At briefing, instructions are given to the bombardier as to intervalometer setting, i.e., how much interval between bombs. Long intervals with a high number of bombs seems to take forever and can be excruciating depending on the fire you're taking.

As stated the normal altitude for medium bombers was around 11, 500 feet altitude. The lead box was slightly higher than the second as was each of its flights. Bad feeling to be the low man in the low box because you are the last one over the target and by then if they were going to get good, they were going to get good at you. On one occasion while in the slot the plane on our left took a direct hit. I could not see it from my vantage point but I knew of it. It was carrying some "Observers" from a ground unit (Infantry, Tank?) flying with us to understand air operations. Idea was that we in turn sent aircrews to be in on ground operations up close. Some air crews who did this rode with a tank crew going through some German town with their guns traversed left and right firing away. Thankfully this was discontinued before I had this "Opportunity." Not sure but the direct hit I mentioned may have keeled this practice.

These German 88's usually were in four-gun batteries and it was not unusual to have these black blossoms (imagine a black rose) suddenly show up when you didn't expect it. Ordinarily when we were briefed we knew where the flak belts were, or were told, and tried to go straight across them and not fly down one of them. Because then they could really get on you. It was also not unusual to realize that they were very close to you, and just as you would do evasive action and turn left or right there would be a four-gun burst off just to your side. Sometimes they didn't miss. If it was close, you could feel it and you could hear it and you could smell it—that cordite smell to it. If it should hit your airplane, which was not uncommon—knock a hole in it, it sounded like being inside of a drum. Of course if it was a major hit you were going down, and luckily that never happened to me. I do recall on one of the early missions seeing up ahead one of the airplanes was on fire, apparently the engine had been hit and he was going down. I remember thinking how very bright that fire was. At that time we were looking for parachutes, and I really don't recall whether there were any or not. On returns after bombing the Group flew at 210 IAS although on occasion if a dive was initiated during evasive action 210 could be well exceeded.

Ordinarily we were six days on ops and two days off. Occasionally a max effort raid would be called during a surge or major defensive action and the entire group would go, 54 airplanes in all. Our squadron commander was a Lt. Col. J. B. Smith from Kansas. Young but experienced having flown 26s in the Aleutians or Alaska. He was sort of a long, tall type fellow. I can remember him sort of hunched over smoking a cigarette, walking along, and showing his Kansas upbringing because he had a real farmer's walk. Behind his back he was referred to as "Dirt Track Smith." However, I don't think anyone called him this to his face. He was killed at 26 or 27. Our flight leader, which was the guy who would normally be in lead of a six airplane flight, was a Lt. Humphreys, who I believe had been an English professor at Baylor University before the war. Humphreys also was a fast man with a bottle as many were who had been too long at it. It was not unusual to have some hard drinkers in the outfit. If you weren't one when it started, you might become one before you got through. I remember Humphrey as being unusual looking because his teeth were sort of like fence pickets—they had space between them.

Our ranking officer's group level and squadron level, usually Lt. Colonels or Colonels, did fly with us and lead flights. However, I got assigned to another squadron after the war and found out that not everyone did this. Their squadron commander flew a P47 up to the bomb line and then stopped and waited for them to come back. Not bad but not much of an example to his men. Given a choice, I would probably have done likewise.

One thing I do remember when we first got to Great Saling was going to town there. We had heard of the blackout, but nothing like what there was there, because we immediately got lost and had to link arms to get back, and then I ran into a pole. Because when they said blackout, they meant blackout.

We were also under buzz bomb attack quite often. These were German V1 buzz bombs which used a pulse jet engine on a small pilotless aircraft. Germans would either fly them in launched out of occupied France or bring them in at night mounted on top of a Heinkel Bomber and launch them. These things did tremendous damage to London. In fact, at one time it was classified—not allowed to say just how much damage was being done by them. But they would come in at night flying very, very low—right over your head. One time I thought one of them was going to light right on top of me, when really it was just an Army truck. But I thought Buzz Bomb and when their engine cut off they dove in and exploded. I remember picking up my helmet with eggs in it and putting it on my head. (Combat crews got three fresh eggs a week.) Antiaircraft could knock these things down if they could get to them, since they were usually low and flew very fast—I think close to 400 mph, fast at the time. However, the English would come down with Hawker Typhoons, a rather strong airplane—pretty fast—dive at them and get right up right next to them and tip the wings and cause them to tumble. Sort of an exciting way to shoot one down, but better than trying to shoot at them.

Some English airfields had the DREM system for night or fog landing. These were lights on poles around their airfields in sort of an elliptical shape leading in to the runway. The only problem was that these lights had been set up some years before when the airplanes were much slower and could make that turn. It could not be done in an aircraft of B26 class because it would be quite dangerous to make a turn like that at night in black that close to the ground.

As you might expect, life in some of the Nissan huts did get to be pretty rowdy sometimes. Crews could get pretty fractious, raising hell in general. Sometimes the entire hut would be held up or restricted to quarters and not allowed to go into town. Although they were not prevented from flying their combat duty. When that happened, they were usually confined until one of the members of the hut got shot down. At that time, someone would go down very piously and tell the Colonel that poor old so-and-so was the one that made all the noise and raised the ruckus. With that he would be commended for having come in and told on the lost malefactor and everybody would be released from confinement. One group of poker players suffered the wrath of one of the losing players when he climbed up on the top of the hut and removing the smokestack urinated on the playing table. Bedlam.

Shortly before I joined this squadron, our group tried night bombing. This was disastrous and the English who specialized in night bombing had some people come over and talk with them. They were told your aircraft are not really equipped for night flying because you don't have the right instruments. The English didn't understand why, because they were American instruments that the RAF had. The 322nd tried night bombing anyway. Mistake. The Group went in right at the time that the German night fighters were following RAF Lancasters returning from a night raid, picked up on the B26s and a lot of them were shot down. The Germans then got on the radio and broadcast back saying "Nye's Annihilators were annihilated last night"—Col. Nye at that time being the group commander.

We also used to listen after someone was shot down because the Germans would quite often come on and announce prisoners of war. Sometimes it would be hard to believe when you've seen an airplane explode or go down how anyone could have lived, but sometimes they did. And the Germans did usually tell it right as to who they had captured.

There was never an American bombing raid turned back because of enemy fire, but I understand that during the terrible losses they had with the night flights that some of the people did intentionally get too drunk to fly. I guess it was a pretty terrible thing. Luckily they had stopped night bombing by the time I got in the squadron. (Time and propinquity in. my favor again.) Occasionally you would get back from a mission after dark. And that could be pretty hairy, trying to get a whole group in when many of them were running low on fuel.

Naturally being a new crew we were initially broken up and put in with experienced people on our early flights. I remember my first flight was with a Lt. Coffman, who allegedly had been an RAF pilot—an American in the RAF—before, and then crossed over to the American Air Force. We got in and took off, not much said. And he got up to altitude and says, "You got it." He was flying as deputy lead, which is number four—the slot right underneath the lead airplane. I had never flown that position in the States and remember wallowing around with it trying to get the hang of it. Actually, once you got it, it wasn't too difficult to fly, but you're flying all the time looking up with your head tilted back, all the time looking up at the airplane ahead and above you. And you are quite close to him. In any event, I got to where I could fly the position, went all the way to the target, bombed—I was still flying—came back—still flying—getting ready to let down in formation through the overcast and I was tired and not really up for this. (Never had tried this before.) I chickened out and started calling for him to come get this thing. He came back up and took over and flew in and landed it. After we were on the hardstand, stopped, he said, "How many missions you have?" I said, "This was the first." He says, "What?! Why didn't you say so?" I said, "Well, you didn't ask." And on top of that I was new and didn't want to say anything. I ran into him many years later (he is dead now) at a reunion. I asked him if he remembered this. He said, "Yes, I do." And I said, "Well, what were you thinking anyway?" He said, "Well," he says, "I looked at you and you looked like you could fly all right. So I just let you do it. Besides that, I wanted to see the bombs fall. I never had seen the bombs fall. So I went back and watched out of the bomb bay to see them fall and hit. After that it seemed pretty good to just sit in the radio room and fly around." Although it was rather nerve wracking for me, it did give me great confidence. And we later flew that position often with Dewey as a deputy lead. I got to like it pretty well.

There was one of the dangers of night flying that was brought on with sad results that occurred when a B24 group was coming in elsewhere in England after dark. Germans came up in JU88s, which was a fast twin-engine airplane, joined the pattern and shot down some of the B24s, before anyone knew who they were. Great war.

Outbound in Armor

BOMBING
MISCELLANY

Each airplane carried 4,000 pounds of bombs. We could carry two 2,000 pounders, four 1,000 pounders, eight 500 pounders, or I believe as much as sixteen 250 pound bombs. All of this depended on the target. The 2,000 pounders were for heavy large bridges. The 500 pounders or 1,000 pounders could be for fortified sites and of course on down to 250 were more or less fragmentation type or anti-personnel bombs.

On one occasion, we bombed with little 50 pound frag bombs (each about the size of a medium thermos bottle) arranged in a bomb rack in an assembly of nine of these little frag bombs assembled in a triangular grouping of three in line to a rack. I think we carried 8 Or 9 racks of these little jewels. When a rack dropped, the frags came loose, as a 45 caliber bullet fired through the middle of a pipe around which the groups of three were arranged, thus cutting the wires holding the bombs together and they all came out like confetti. The only time we dropped these provided a near disaster. Borst was flying, deputy lead, in the slot. As copilot I could see ahead and see these little frags coming out like confetti. Of course he was flying and looking up at the lead airplane holding in position. As these things came out I could see some hit each other, and some hitting airplanes. In fact one airplane was already on fire in its engine where one of these things had gone into the engine. Noticing this and knowing this was going to happen just as the airplane ahead of us dropped, I remember yanking up on the control yoke. Dewey thought I had gone crazy, But what I was trying to do was get us up out of that crap that was falling back. As it was, the rack that held those little bombs rattled along the bottom of our airplane, otherwise it could have come right into the cockpit with us. Lead airplane prop wash almost turned us over as my pulling up put us right into the lead airplane's strip stream but it was the only thing to do.

Upon return we learned that the armament officer had failed to tell us we were supposed to uncover when we dropped these little frags. Only time we ever dropped them.

Our defensive armament included 11 50-caliber machine guns. One flexible gun in the bombardier's compartment in the nose; four "package guns," two on each side of the fuselage fixed and firing forward; two in the top turret, two in the tail turret and two firing out of each side of the waist openings . We all wore flak jackets and flak helmets over the bomb line. Some put a flak jacket in the pilot or copilot's seat and one bombardier lined his nose compartment lined with flak jackets to the extent that the plane was nose heavy. Exaggeration? The pilot had a sort of steel sarcophagus he could slide his seat back in to if he was not flying while the copilot had a flat steel sheet behind him.

There is a museum outside Savannah for the Eighth Air Force where they have a simulated bombing run which is very realistic. When bombs fall out if they are any size each time one falls you can feel your pants leg flutter from the wind. This museum is set up so that the simulated bombing run has the same feel because they give you a puff of air and it makes you just jump because it's just exactly like it felt when bombs fell out. We also dropped incendiary bombs. As I recall individually a couple of inches in diameter and maybe 2 feet long and they really came out in a container and then separated and fell like matchsticks. We would carpet the target with these magnesium bombs and once they hit they stuck and ignited the target. However most of our targets were marshaling yards or railroads and bridges and occasionally fortified positions with armor or troops and sometimes towns where there were crossroads. Sad to say sometime aiming points were church steeples as they are good aiming points. In bombing Magdeburg we just set the town up in grid coordinates and everybody took a grid and bombed in trying to destroy the town. This was because the town was allegedly full of German troops. Sad to say however, I understand Magdeburg was a very historical city but maybe no more.

From here on I guess you could call this a stream of consciousness or a stream of memory because up until now I have tried to be in phases of flight training and across the ocean and things of that nature but from here on I just remember things which may or may not have happened in the order presented but they are things that come back as I write this. I'll try to place them in a particular time that I can refer to or otherwise it's just something that happened.

In case of emergency the Bombardier can salvo the bombs, meaning when you salvoed, you dropped all at one time. This would be if you lost an engine, been hit and in trouble and going to jump or going down.

We did have one fellow that was shot down on a blind bombing raid (G box bombing through the clouds). The Germans knew of these G boxes but I don't think they knew for sure how they worked. When captured he was a Bombardier but got identified by his also captured pilot as a Navigator. (These were the people that operated G boxes.) The Germans kept him in solitary confinement for about 6 weeks trying to find out how the thing worked. When he came back I ran into him after he was released. He stated that after staying in solitary confinement he tried to make up things because he really didn't know anything about the G box, but because he was so tired of being in confinement, he was getting stir crazy. Eventually they let him out finally deciding maybe he didn't know anything, which he didn't.

Another thing that would happen when you were doing blind bombing was down below and in front we would fly three airplanes running a window mission. These three would be doing big lazy eights throwing out aluminum, strips of aluminum designed to blind the German radar firing through the clouds by radar. Window missions were supposed to be a pretty good mission as they usually wouldn't shoot at you when they had the big target of a whole group behind you to shoot at. But the time we flew one I remember them damned well shooting at us. On top of that we had a rather excitable radio operator, Papas, and he got very excited and threw out all the aluminum too fast. Pretty soon we were down at a lower altitude by ourselves with no window going out. Easy target then.

I remember Papas because he was of Greek origin and a radio operator to begin with. He went through a lengthy training course in radio. But when we got overseas they took that type of radio out of the airplane and he became a waist gunner which was really all that we had for him to do. By then we had very good VHF communications. We could call and get directions to the nearest clear field if lost. You could call Parade, "hello Parade, give me a course to steer to the nearest clear field." Then a WAC would come on, and ask for a short count; you responded with one, two, three, four, five, four, three, two, one, and she would come back with a heading directing you to the nearest clear airfield. This was in the event you got separated from your Group which did occasionally happen.

The D Day invasion had occurred and troops were moving on. The battle of Germany was about to begin and we were identified to move over on the continent to an airfield in France. We were to fly to our new field at Beauvais France north of Paris.

Getting ready to go was quite an undertaking. We were going into the field and were to prepare accordingly. Everyone was told to prepare a full field pack. Now none of us in the Air Force has ever seen a full field pack because that was not our training. Someone finally found a field manual that had a picture of a field pack in it so all of us constructed, and I do mean constructed one that looked like it. It was stuck together and I don't think it could have been opened with a can opener. Nevertheless we all had" full field packs." We were also issued canvas legging to put on as if we were going to be walking around in a swamp. Immediately people began to cut half of them off so it looked more like a paratrooper.

That set the Colonel off. We had damaged government property. Hell was raised over that but there was not much he could do about it. When I say not much could be done about things, remember when you are in a combat situation already, there is not a whole lot they can do to you. Yes they can maybe make life miserable for you but you are going to keep flying anyway.

Finally the great day came when we were getting ready to move out of England and our Executive Officer, Major Root, had everybody fall out. I think we went by crews which meant there were six people lined up: pilot, copilot, on back through the six man crew. We all had our home made field packs on, looking good. Not. Root was looking around trying to get everyone there and about that time our flight leader, Humphreys, finally showed up late for the formation on a bicycle. It was one of those bicycles that had a covered skirt on the rear wheel. He had taken what looked like a pinetop and written "Hump" on it to identify it as his. When he showed up he had no sign of a field pack but had only a musette bag. Major Root, the Executive Officer, had a small tantrum and said what have you got in that musette bag? Humphreys may have been slightly under the influence, when he opened it up. He had a towel and a quart of whisky. Well that didn't go over too well. Shortly after that, Farcus, who was the Squadron Bombardier; a big fellow, showed up wearing an ammunition belt with a ring of canteens all filled up with lemon juice mix so he would have something to mix with whisky when he got to where he was going. When finally assembled Major Root gave the order to "open ranks," which is ordinarily done only four people deep. It couldn't be done with six and some people snickered and some laughed and that really set him off. We finally got through with this, mounted up and got in the airplanes and off we went carrying everybody's belongings as well as the pseudo field packs. The idea was that our ground crews and our ground personnel were supposed to be there when we got there as they had already left. In true World War II fashion they got there six weeks later.

We were there pretty much alone in Beauvais in what had been a German airfield. The French looked at us askance when they saw that we were using the runways. "Well the Germans didn't use the runways, they were not any good," and used the highway for take offs and landings. But those were fighters, not bombers.

I don't know if you read the book *Catch-22*, but if you have, I sometimes think I was in that group. Maybe not quite as bad as that but many of the things in that book were all too believable. But we could fly, fly well, and hit targets. The field had individual hard stands for the planes which were not parked together. One fellow in the Squadron, an old timer named Carmody, a little short fellow, pulled up on his hard stand as an old French lady was standing there. In sort of broken English asked, "Are you American?" "Yes." "You American fly airplane?" "Yes, I fly airplane." "You bomb this place?" "Oh yea, I bombed everywhere." She walked up and slapped him. So much for talking big to someone you may have just bombed. Although the French were not living immediately amongst us, they lived in and around there. Luckily it wasn't a German. They would have probably stuck him with a pitchfork.

Speaking of pitchforks and Germans, that really did happen fairly often. I couldn't tell you how many, I know that we had three chute failures in our squadron, More about that later. One of the fellows was identified as having fallen with a failed chute and killed had really been killed on the ground by German farmers. Word was put out that his chute had failed in order to not let his family know that he had really been lynched on the ground. This could happen to people and we found out later it happened more than we thought. I guess you can understand that people who are being bombed didn't take too kindly when somebody floated down in a parachute in the middle of them. On the other hand some German civilians reacted with kindness to injured airmen. Case in point was Hopkins's crew. They were returning having failed to bomb and still bomb laden. They had let down having fallen behind and were at about 3000 feet when Flak hit them. Bad navigation I guess because they thought they were over friendly territory but were still over enemy territory. Hopkins the pilot had pushed his seat back and the copilot was flying when they were hit. They went down in a somewhat controlled crash landing .A wing dug in slinging bombs out through the closed bomb bay doors and exploded behind the airplane. All of them badly tossed around. A gunner lost a leg and died on the spot. The first person to arrive was a young German girl about 16. Hopkins was on his back dazed and she pointed to his watch. He said no but she unbuckled it anyway. He said he was too out of it to resist. With that she put it in his shirt pocket and buttoned it. When German soldiers arrived they took everyone's watch but he kept his. Hopkins was one of the lucky ones. he went from 2nd Lt to captain almost overnight. He had just been promoted to first Lt when shot down. But as a prisoner he was due a promotion so he went to Captain. He and the crew were put in a German hospital. The German Doctor, realizing that the war was close to over and being almost surrounded, told them we can't treat you and will try and get you back. The doctor and two German GIs took them down to the banks of the Rhine, waved a white flag and yelled across. With that someone shot at them and Hopkins said he thought it was a no go. But shortly under a white flag two American paratroopers came over to get them. The two German GIs wanted to go too, but the Doctor said he needed them and wouldn't let them go. True story. I've been on the Rhine at that spot and it is clearly close enough to make the call.

Parachutes in the states are very well kept up and repacked I believe every several weeks, two months, or something like that. In England chutes were kept separate and kept in pristine condition and repacked periodically. However, when we got over on the continent they said we can't do that anymore, we'll have all the chutes in one tent or you can take your chute and keep it with you. As it was very damp and there was not going to be much chance of being repacked or anything else, I kept mine with me and most of us did to be sure that it was in good condition. This notwithstanding, there were two people who had a true chute failure. One being a guy whose shroud lines parted on him when the strap that held the harness together parted and down he went. Another who did survive but he had a chest type packet that would not open and he tom it open with his hands tearing his fingernails almost off but he did survive. One fellow had insisted on having an old seat type parachute. Most of us that were pilots had backpacks which fit close to your back, in fact, mine rubbed a spot on my back and I think I can still find the spot. But he insisted on an old type seat pack that we flew back in training. He would have never been able to get out of the airplane he found out. He had to make a crash landing later and of course everybody jumped out and he still had that chute on and when he tried to get out he got caught and couldn't get out. He did get out by getting out of the chute and leaving it in the airplane. It made a Christian out of him as far as wearing a backpack.

One of our area missions that I recall vividly was to Mulhouse Gap in an area which we thought of as the south of France. I don't know if it was south but it was south to us. We were told there was only a four gun flak battery down below and not to worry about it too much. People that tell you that are not going on the mission, you are. We got a lot of fire from that four gun battery, the reason being they were mounted up on a mountain and we were not too much higher than the mountain to begin with. We did survive but it made me cautious of: what people told us on mission planning.

If we were going on a mission the next day, the alert list was posted on a bulletin board, typed up, stating who was flying and what airplane, what flight and position in the squadron, and who was flying with who as well as who was leading. After that, you immediately knew that you were going in the morning. Early on the Tannoy started up, which is a British name for the PA system. I think it stood for "Too Annoy," because it did. It first called lead crews, to an earlier briefing, maybe as early as 3:00 or 3:30 in the morning. Then the rest of the crews were called in later in the morning. It could be quite early. My memory is walking in the dark, head down in a black void trying to feel your way to the briefing room. Sometimes you had the feeling that this is never going to end. Briefing was held in a room with a big map, usually covered at first and then uncovered and with a colored string showing where you are going and the target. There could be a lot of oo's and ah's and a few well laced profane statements. Or it could be a milk run and people could laugh and talk about it; lots of nervous laughter in any event. There is also notice of where the flak concentrations are and your route to try to fly across them. Fighter escort rendezvous (if any) is set. However, if it is an antipersonnel target where you are in close and you don't want to drop on your troops, you are going to have to fly down that line to be sure that the bombs do not fall on your own troops. This was all well and good however it was not unusual to have delays where the Tannoy would say, "One-hour delay, one-hour delay." Several hours might go by while you sit around on the "ready" waiting to go. Finally you might go and then again the thing might be stood down. This could be weather is too bad, target change, or what have you. Our life in the flying Air Force was something like that all the time. You were either out being shot at, behind that German lines, maybe hundreds of miles bombing and then you came back to relative peace and calm and slept in a cot at night. It was sort of a hot cold type of thing; great stress in between and then a calm. Some people stood this better than others and I guess I did since nothing happened to me. But some did get totally bonkers after a while.

A long mission for us was five-hours. Occasionally we went on two in one day which is exhausting. In fact, by then you are so tired that you don't really care if you get hit or not. But you know you are going, it's posted and you know it and are awakened early. We were told once that the French had asked us to bomb some place that was too close for comfort. We told them we are fearful of hitting their people. They said, "Well that's all right, we'll lose some anyway." Cold blooded bunch. We didn't do it anyway as I understand. This was only hearsay and maybe not true.

When we first got to France we were given a little pup tent which really was not long enough for me to sleep in. We were on the ground at first and we didn't have sleeping bags. There was a field hospital being set up across the field from us. It was not occupied yet so a group of us went over and stole cots from them.

I got the cot back and it wouldn't fit into a pup tent unless you dug the cot down into the ground. But even then part of it stuck out the end. I got in it and then realized it was raining on my feet which were sticking out the end even though under a blanket. I then pulled out my gas cover, a plastic sack which was for gas protection and we never had to use them. I got up in the middle of the night and put that thing over the foot of the cot and made out at least for the time being.

One small piece of humor (humorous??) broke the monotony right after we moved to Beauvais. Our Chaplain was a Captain and had a very large dog. Lieutenant Colonel Smith, the Squadron Commander, had a small dog. In the midst of all the other excitement, etc., going on during the war, these two dogs met up. A vicious dog fight ensued and of course the large dog got the best of it. When it looked as though it would be terminal, Colonel Smith came out of his tent, saw what was happening, and shot the chaplain's dog with his 45, killing it. This set off a real brouhaha with the Colonel going back inside his tent and the Chaplain, the Captain, standing outside challenging him to come outside and fight. Eventually cooler heads prevailed and nothing came of it but it did provide a little excitement for those of us standing around looking. Secretly I think we really hoped they would fight.

There was a German ammunition dump across the way from us and some of us went over there and got boxes that had incendiary bombs in them. Threw them out and brought boxes home and made a little field chest out of it. Looking back that was probably stupid, it could have been booby trapped. When you are young and invincible (armed with an invincible ignorance I always said), nothing bothers you too much.

We had the usual flight surgeon, Captain Wheeler, who spent most of his time telling us he was really too good to be dealing with people like us and he ought to be back at a base hospital somewhere. Luckily he had a Tech Sergeant assistant who really did most of the medication. Wheeler's main talent seemed to be to drink up the whisky ration that we got. That was a thing called a "NAAFI" ration which from the British where they got so much booze for the squadron. NAAFI—Navy/Army/Air Force/Institute? The idea was that you got a shot of booze when you got back from the mission. As I recall, he drank up the good stuff and what he wound up with for us was rum or something strange. He also could really put it away and one night when we were in bigger pyramidal tents, he fell down out in the mud between two of the tents. We went out, myself and another Lieutenant, and tried to pick him up as he was lying in the mud. He said, "Unhand me, you enlisted men." So we just dropped him and left him there. He was still there in the morning. It's a wonder he didn't die of pneumonia.

One of the pastimes when you were not flying, was to go out and watch as the Group came home. You knew what time it was coming in so you would go out and count the airplanes to see how many made it and how many didn't. Sort of a gallows pastime but that was one of the things that we did. Also on one occasion the Group apparently got lost in weather and none came in. We thought everybody had been lost at first but some slowly came in and others had landed all over France. In fact, one had bombed a bridge in Switzerland. The first thing we knew of that was when staff cars full of brass began to arrive looking for the guilty party. The Swiss were extremely neutral. So neutral that they would come up and shoot you down if they got the chance so we tried to give them a wide berth. They flew Me109s.

The aircraft *Flak-Bait* (now in the Smithsonian) was in our Group but not in my Squadron. On its 200th mission some big wig came down to fly and lead the group because it was the 200th mission flown by that plane. I was on that particular mission and I can remember that lead person saying, "Deputy, take the lead" and he dropped back and became Deputy. We didn't know why. Before we got home though he had called the armament officer, the engineering officer, this guy and that guy and anyone else he could think of to meet that airplane. I guess he then raised holy hell because it turned out that that *Flak-Bait* had never been flown as a lead and the newly installed bomb site was not hooked up. Consequently, General Bull Moose was unable to take credit for leading the 200th *Flak-Bait* mission.

One event out of that time when everybody got lost, a Lieutenant Griswold, a little short stocky pilot from Tennessee, copilot was Gilbert, had made a forced landing in a French field. They got it on the ground but it was such a short field that there was some question if they could take off again. The next day they went back to the airplane and got as much gear as they could off of it and gave it a go. The field had a low little stone fence at one end of this cow pasture. Griswold ran the engines up wide open, bled the flaps and away they went wide open until they got almost to the fence and Gilbert popped the flaps and up the thing rose (levitated) over the stone fence and he got home with it. For this I think he got the Distinguished Flying Cross. I guess he earned it.

He did miss one thing however when on leave in Paris. He was in a department store and this female who he thought was too pushy came up and tried to strike up a conversation with him. He told her to get the hell away or something like that. Thought she was a street walker. It turned out it was Marlene Dietrich who was over there as a Goodwill Ambassador.

We once bombed a bridge at Trier, which is a beautiful part of the country. However the Germans had an anti-aircraft school there we were told and they really made it hot for us. I don't know if we lost airplanes or not but I know we got a lot of flak. We dropped 2000 pound bombs on that bridge and got a hit, at least someone in the flight got hits because it had big round holes punched in it. Sadly the fuse was set wrong or something of that nature and consequently we had to go back another day to knock that bridge down.

In the midst of all the carnage, confusion and chaos which were going on in World War II, I did experience one morning a very beautiful sight. This occurred on a weather flight which I flew with a pilot by the name of Rusty Kusluch. As an aside, Kusluch was killed right after the war while flying in a German trainer plane. Stupid accident; he and another friend of mine, George Gaudette, had taken it out to check it out and some way managed to crash and kill both of them. Don't know how I happened to be flying with Kusluch, but I was. In any event, we were to check weather to see whether or not it was satisfactory for a mission that was going out that day. We took off in lousy weather; practically solid clocks (instruments) from Beauvais, France, early in the morning, long before daylight. The weather officer told us that we had a fair ceiling (it didn't look like that when we took off) with low scud clouds, ground fog, and a heavy overcast. I remember passing the red warning light on Beauvais Cathedral as soon as we took off flying on instruments. However, when we broke through the clouds on top, I don't know how high we were, must have been 8,000-10,000 feet maybe, I saw what has to have been the most beautiful memorable scene I have ever seen. I am 82 now and have since flown literally thousands of miles and hours commercially while working some 30 years as a Boeing Engineer and have never seen anything like it. What we saw was day barely breaking. From the east the sun was just peeping over the clouds and the overcast sky was a ripple of gold as the sun's ray struck the cloud tops. As we turned, the moon was going down in the west and literally appeared green with the tops of clouds in that direction, being an iridescent green. We both commented on it at the time. It lasted only a little while but I have never forgotten it and I am sure he would not either had he lived. I have never seen anything remotely like it since. Needless to say, when we got back on the ground metro people told us that it looked like we had a clear view through the overcast, meaning they could look through a hole. Think the mission went any way. So much for a weather flight.

As the allies were getting ready to cross the Rhine we were on a bombing run and we could look down and see the artillery fire going both ways It was late afternoon and looked like 10,000 fire flies down there, all heavy artillery firing at each other. As we were coming out the RAF was coming in. The RAF flying Lancasters did not seem to fly in formation. They just flew in a cluster that looked like a cartoon bunch of bees or something coming. They would fly right through your formation so you had to give way for them. They went in like that and put a master bomber up in the air over a city and then called in bombers. Whereas they felt we were sort of crazy for daylight bombing and we knew they were crazy for the night bombing.

> Who could see the bomber crews without admiring the phlegmatic determination which makes other kinds of courage seem no more than temporary lapses of judgment? They were the real heroes, the ones who came up here day after day as human targets for every weapon an ingenious, dedicated, and tenacious foe could use against them. So in life itself the true measure of courage is to fly on despite the tragedies of accident, sickness, or failure.
> —Deighton, *Goodbye Mickey Mouse*

Sitting around on the ground when you are not flying or weathered in is a pretty dull experience. The dullest and most dreadful task of all was to censor mail. We would be on the ground for a week or so and they would come in with a big tub full of mail which we had to go through and censor for all the enlisted men. I don't remember what we did, but ours (officer mail) must have been censored too. I remember getting these letters and reading, and believe me reading other people's mail has got to be the absolute dullest, worst thing on earth. This was with the exception of one rather fat and fortyish red faced, bald headed, Sergeant Hawk. Sergeant Hawk would write some of the most lurid letters home to his wife that those of us only 20 years old and unmarried had never heard of (or imagined) anything like that. We also knew from his letters that he carried on quite a love life on the side and we always did try to get Sergeant Hawk's letters because they were always great. There were others who were ground crew and about as safe as you could be but they would write letters home about dodging bullets and how bad everything was. I would think, God, this isn't happening but that's what they were writing home.

For lack of anything else to do I used to play penny-ante poker. We had two games going in the squadron. Penny-ante was where you might lose a couple of dollars and I played in that one because I learned a long time ago that if you win all of my money, I will kill you. Show me a good loser and I'll show you a loser. They did have another table where the guys played for serious money and kept the money in a safe when they weren't playing. These guys would play for big stakes. I remember one time they were playing and a mission was called and one of the guys, a Bombardier by the name of Flannagan, was playing but not on the list for the mission. He decided he would go along just for the ride. Damned if the airplane didn't get shot down with him in it. I don't know if he got killed or prisoner but it broke up that particular part of the game for a while anyway.

Another pastime which we had was to chunk knives. We all had been issued a trench knife I suppose in case we got into hand to hand combat which was extremely unlikely. We would stand around and chunk knives at trees in the area until they all looked like they had been worked on by beavers. Where we were was owned by some Frenchman because he used to walk through and count the trees. At night we would slip out with a cross cut saw and cut those trees down for firewood because· it was freezing cold. The winter of 44 was the worst winter we ever had with snow everywhere and we were freezing to death. We would cut those trees down and burn the damn log, split them up and burn then in the little pot bellied stove. The kitchen had briquettes, little coal briquettes which I had never seen before. They were little things that looked like eggs made out of pressed coal. We all had a little pot belly stove in the middle of the tent. We were in those pyramidal tents by then which were not bad quarters. But we would slip down one or two at a time usually when no one was watching and steal those little briquettes because they were better to burn than the wood.

We were undoubtedly not the cleanest bunch of people because for a long time we had no shower facilities at all and we got to be pretty gamey. There was an old man in the army there who had to be 100 and apparently had been drafted. It was his job to run this little two-bit shower arrangement that we had.

But he somehow couldn't run it worth a flip because when they finally got it running you could try to take a shower and it could go from scalding hot to ice cold in a flash and he would just shake his head, didn't know what it was. Once however they did load us all up in trucks and took us to a common bath (Salle de Bain?) in Beauvais. There was a large room of little divided places around the edge and everybody got to take a shower. I don't know when we washed our clothes, although I remember washing underwear in a bucket. We had got some old green boards from a German building that had been painted dark green and I remember putting those things on top of the bucket while we were boiling the clothes. We got green paint all over everything which was a real mess. Luckily all of our underwear was olive drab anyway. Cold as it was I had on regular underwear, then I had long underwear on and my mother had knitted a sleeveless wool sweater and I had that on too. I had a wool uniform over that, high top shoes with regular socks. Then when I flew I sometimes had a flight suit but usually I flew in coveralls, with a leather jacket over that and a fur lined cap with a bill on it. The fur lined cap with a bill on it came in quite handy because if you were not flying and we were taking fire I would pull that cap down so that I couldn't see. However I would keep that down until finally a flak burst gets close to you. But I would keep that cap pulled down under the cockpit looking down, not looking out and invariably you can't stand it and when I'd look up the damn stuff would flash right in my face. We were of course wearing flak jackets we put on once we got over the bomb line. I had a big steel flak helmet also. I tipped my head back once and I didn't have the strap on right and that helmet fell off and rolled back in the radio room. I got up to go back there and could hardly walk due to my flak jacket and about that. time we started getting flak and I had to really scramble to get back up and get my hat on and get back up in the cockpit.

On one occasion Papas got hit-in the chest by a piece of flak and it knocked him down. He had on a flak jacket so it really didn't hurt him. He was ordinarily a dark complexioned fellow but he turned grey-white that day. Once we went across the bomb line going in we had to turn off the cabin heat. Don't ask me why but we did. In any event when we would start back across the line coming out we would pull it on and pretty soon Papas would say, "get me some of that heat, turn the heat on, turn the heat on." We would get it back on and within five seconds he'd get to smelling this burning smell that came out of the heater and he shout, "We're on fire!, We're on fire!" He was pretty excitable.

At the start of a mission we had a little mission bag with an escape kit in it and some maps and a few things like that and a candy bar. The candy bar was supposed to be eaten at the far end of the flight for energy. However, on occasion airplanes did not take off and either aborted or may have even crashed on takeoff. Before I took off I always ate the candy bar figuring if I'm going to roll up in a red ball, I'm going to be with a full gut anyway. We also got five or six candy bars a week in a ration and that really wasn't enough to suit me so I used to eat all of mine at once and was about sick and then didn't want any more candy for a week.

Just about everyone smoked at that time and we also got cigarette rations. You couldn't spend more than about two dollars a week so I really came out of the service with a fair amount of money. We got a cigarette brand I think called Chelsea or something like that and it was publicized as being the GI's favorite. Nobody liked them but they were plentiful. To get rid of them we would put them in a Camel or Chesterfield package and if anyone bummed a cigarette they got a Chelsea in a Camel or Chesterfield package. Otherwise even a bummer wouldn't take them.

Probably the best thing I had in the Army was the dental care that I received. As I stated I was a child of the depression which was not an interesting dental memory. I was well treated, however, in the Army by good dentists. As I mentioned I had one impacted wisdom tooth taken out in Lake Charles. I got another wisdom tooth, really right after the war and I remember being taken over to a Field Hospital or a Field Dental Office in this small German town. My jaw is hurting and I walk in to this dentist office. The first thing I notice was a fellow came in with Captain's bars on his coat and I thought well that's the Dentist and then he took that coat off and he was a Staff Sergeant. Turns out he was the Technician. At that time up showed this officer and it turned out he was the Captain but he had sent the Sergeant over to stand inspection for him. He asked the Sergeant, "Did the old man notice anything?" "No, he just thought I was you." Well I looked at the guy who was doing the work on my teeth and I asked "Is this going to hurt?" and I remember him telling me, "What the hell do I care, it ain't my mouth." Well that was not too heartening but he did fiddle around in there and in a few minutes I guess he was a pretty good dentist because he had given me a shot of Novocain and I remember him saying, "Well don't swallow it stupid, I got it out!" And that was the end of that. But at least I was full of Novocain and about half doped up and was sent outside to sit on this little stone fence. By then there were a lot of Germans that had been captured and turned loose. The war had just ended, and I'm sitting there with my leather jacket on with bombs written all across the back of it trying to not draw attention because I had to wait for my truck to come get me. I was afraid of getting lynched by a bunch of these ex-German soldiers although they seemed pretty well cowed by then. This next event really didn't happen until the war was over in Germany but the war was still going on gangbusters in the Pacific. This was before the A Bomb. We were all getting ready to be shipped over there. Captain Wheeler came through in good form. Word had gone out publicly through a publication in the states, "Don't worry mother, your son will have a complete physical exam before he can be sent over there." I remember we all went down to the mess hall in this orphanage in Belgium where we were quartered. Wheeler came in and said take your shirt off. I remember standing there in my undershirt and him feeling me on both sides of my chest and asking, "You feel all right don't you boy?" and says, "Get up there closer if you can't read that chart. You're all right," and with that "exam" pronounced me okay for flight duty and further overseas assignment. That was the end of my Flight 64 Physical to say that I was prepared and ready to go to the Pacific. The A Bomb short-circuited that.

BEAUVAIS, BATTLE OF THE BULGE, AND BELGIUM

We were bombing all across Europe by now. One of the closest raids we ever made to Berlin was to a town called Jüterbog about 30 miles out. As you got closer to Berlin, the flak would get thicker and thicker because they had rings of flak all around the city. We did not go into Berlin but Jüterbog was close enough. We also flew missions into Czechoslovakia bombing Eger and another town called Cheb. About this time the RAF was using ten-ton blockbuster bombs. These were carried by Lancaster bombers and were so large that the bombers could not close the bomb bay doors but flew with them partly open. The Lancaster was a four engine bomber with a crew of about five. They carried only a pilot, no copilot and had only 30 caliber (.303) guns to defend them. (We were equipped with 50-caliber.) We could hear them going over at night because they flew at night in terrible weather and occasionally you would hear one wind up, apparently due to ice, and go down. One of Bomber (Butcher) Harris' crews. We also had one crash-land alongside the edge of our runway. It was always a hazard as we took off. As we flew in daylight, we would call in targets of opportunity we could see on the ground. While not our target but when we saw a railroad car or something moving called in a target to a relay station called Ripsaw or whatever the call sign was at that time. In no time at all we would see P-47s diving to bomb it. The RAF's ten-ton blockbuster bombs were sometimes dropped on canals. (Lots of German traffic moved by barge by night.) These blockbusters would crack the earth. Then the barges would run aground as the water ran out. P 47's would come in at daylight, strafe and bomb them.

We had several bad accidents at this time. One morning we had a three airplane mid-air collision while forming up for a mission. I knew one of the pilots involved. This was a Lieutenant Shettles from Mississippi. He had been a cadet with me and was now flying as a Pilot. He had apparently been slow getting into formation and his Colonel (Shettles was in our Group but another Squadron) told him get in formation faster or else. This day he was flying in I believe the left hand position, right off the lead pilot. As he came in, he came in too fast, threw up a wing to slow down and mushed right into the number four airplane (deputy lead in the slot where we flew in our Squadron). Those two blew up along with the lead (third) airplane. The only one to survive was the Pilot of the lead airplane. He reported that all he remembered was holding the controls when he was apparently blown out and his chute blown open. He said that all he could recall was that he was sitting at the controls and then hanging in his parachute looking down at green fields. The ambulances for the three crews were really a mess. That particular Pilot later went over and talked a P47 Group into letting him take a P47 up. (This was not unheard of, our Ops officer Major Sebille was alleged to have done this in England when he took his days off operational status and flew Spitfires with a Polish squadron.) This fellow was flying rather low over our field and shortly thereafter we heard that he had crashed. He was reported to be sitting there in a burning airplane dead in the cockpit turning into a barbecue. Nobody could get to him.

I had one mission when I flew with a Pilot on his own first-pilot-mission. This was Gilbert who had been a longtime copilot and on this occasion I was assigned as his copilot. I don't know which of us were the most nervous.

The Battle of the Bulge was one of the great battles of World War II in Europe. It started December the 16th, 1944 when the Germans came through what was a quiet sector in the Ardennes

Forest on the German/Belgian border. We had green Army divisions there with the exception of the 2nd Division there for a breather in what was supposed to be a quiet area. On the 16th three German armies approximating 500,000 men began an assault on a front of some 50 or 60 miles eventually opposed by 600,000 American and 55,000 British soldiers. The German salient extended into Belgium about 50 miles before being stopped. In an area of a triangle with 50 miles to a side about a million soldiers were engaged. I have read that their intent was to reach the port of Antwerp, cut allied forces in two and force peace talks. Hitler was beginning to see the end. Finally stopped mainly by General Patton's ability to turn his entire American third army in only a few days and come in on the flank of the German offensive. Most casualties occurred in the early part of the battle which continued until January 25th, 1945. German casualties were 100,000, American 81000 and 1400 British. American casualties were the highest of any battle in World War II. British newspapers gave credit to Montgomery, the British Field Marshall, but even he credited Patton.

Weather was terrible: Air Forces were grounded until December the 23rd. That's when it started for us. We seemed to be in the air constantly. I show missions on December 18th, 23rd (2), 24th, 25th (2), 26th, 29th, January 1, 2, 5, 14th, 16th, and the 22nd.

We did not usually have to deal with fighters too much as they usually went after the Heavy bombers. But they made an exception for us at this time. On December 23rd the German Air Force came out in great strength and hit the mediums. One Group, the 394th, another B26 outfit, was hit especially hard. They shot down the leads and deputy leads in the Group, and then while everybody was milling around they picked them off like chickens. I believe they shot down 16 or about half of the Group. After that, we were so shot up that all of the B26 groups had to send people back to England to get more airplanes. With my luck, I didn't get to go to England. I can remember Foil, our flight engineer, was one of the people who went back and came back with a picture of him sitting next to some Red Cross girl making goo-goo eyes.

Fortunately (for me), unfortunately for others, there were two missions on December 23rd and the first mission was the one that was badly hit. As I say fortunately for me I was on the second. I believe we were bombing a bridge at Euskirchen in Germany. I flew that afternoon and got back without too much difficulty. Our Squadron had a very unusual occurrence during this time. I did not see it but it was reported by members of our Squadron that were eye witnesses. A German Me109 fighter popped up right in the middle of a six-ship Flight and could not be shot at as gunners would hit our other ships. He casually looked left and right and then dropped away. He was either curious about B26s or was a senior guy showing off to younger men. At that time Germans had penetrated quite deeply. I believe it was Christmas Eve that the group came back badly shot up with airplanes on single engine and other kinds of battle damage over the field. Pilots were allowing some of their crew that wanted to jump. The airplanes were so badly shot up they were fearful they would crash on landing. The pilot and copilot would stay in and fly right over adjacent to the runway and let their crew bail out.

During the Battle of the Bulge there were rumors of German paratroops in the area. We had deep snow on the ground and when the wind was right we could hear the artillery. Plans were in progress as we might have to move out if the Germans kept coming. I had guard duty, officer of the guard one night, and had to make the rounds to check with all the people who were posted as guards to different airplanes. At this time people were very nervous and trigger happy. I recall once trying to walk on the taxiway to the next airplane and was challenged by the guard on duty. After giving the password, he said, "Approach." I started to· walk around on the hard surface, which would be an easier way to walk and he said, "No sir, walk straight through here." And since he was holding a rifle on me I had to walk across this snow that was waist deep. I remember that quite well. Later there was a car parked in a place that it should not have been, where there usually weren't cars. I couldn't see anyone in it but thought there might be. With my 45-automatic drawn, hammer back, slipping up on the back of that car because I couldn't yell at anybody and couldn't chance waiting for help. It was really sort of a remote place. I edged up from behind with that cocked 45-automatic and almost shot what was moving in the back seat. It turned out to be a large German Shepherd dog and no one in the driver's seat. It turned out to be the Frenchman who owned some of that land who would come through there at night and count the trees. Because we would saw them down at night he would come through the next day or that night and count them and as I understand was charging the US Army for the trees we were chopping down to make firewood. This had apparently been a battleground during World War I because I remember the trees had a lot of shrapnel in them. When you were sawing, you would always be hitting metal.

We did have an air raid alert one night (which didn't materialize, think it was German recon) with all hightailing it to our one dug out bomb shelter. Really sort of a pit with some cover on it. Being among the first there I kept moving back, head down, wondering if anything was going to happen. Suddenly I felt a cold sharp stick at the base of my neck—imagination took over, parachutists in the area, he's stuck his trench knife against my neck, remain silent, is that blood running down my back? No word. Finally I could stand it no more, gently put my hand back there on an icicle hanging down from the roof. Ice stalagtite. Merde!!

Several of my tent mates got a pass in to Paris. This required class A uniforms which we had hung up in the back of the tent under a gas mask cover. When they got them out the rats had eaten the back out of some of them. Panic borrowing set in. Luckily mine had escaped this treatment.

I remember going on leave to Paris and wandering around by myself. I ran on to an old wine shop I guess you would call it. I went in and this old Frenchman was delighted to see an American. I started to buy something and I don't remember what it was. He said, "No, no, not good enough, follow me." We went down about three levels in the basement and I was beginning to get uneasy. I thought well he is probably going to knock me in the head or something. Also, we knew that in the city of Paris there were thousands of German soldiers there who had just decided to hell with the war and stayed; shacked up with some babe. They never gave any trouble but they were there. We knew that they were hidden around. We got all the way down, about three levels into the basement of this old building and the guy dug around in some dust and brought out a bottle of 1914 Cognac. Now at that time most of us would drink most anything, and I carried this back. I was at least smart enough to know that this was probably very valuable. I kept it about three weeks then we all drank it up one night. I'm sure that was pearls before swine because most of us did not have a clue as to what we were drinking. At this time also a fellow came back with a Jerry can full of something and gave everybody a drink. To this day I can remember the thing burning my throat going down. Then it hit my chest and felt like a great giant vise was put on it. I couldn't breathe for a minute or two.

On February 22nd, we were briefed on our part of Operation Clarion--in which all available British and American planes were to strafe and bomb the German transportation system, the idea being that this might bring an end to the war sooner rather than later. About 9000 sorties were flown on the 22nd and 23rd. Our briefing officer was one of three Smiths in the squadron (the other two were our colonel, described previously, and a fellow from White River Junction, Vermont--more on him later). Captain "Smokey" Smith (I don't remember his first name) came in and told us you're all going to get a chance to do what you want to do today. With that he said, "You are going to go down on deck, low-level." (Shades of the memorable Ijmuiden raid!) This was to be a raid to frighten the German railway workers. Don't know who was the most frightened. I remember all of us were pretty well concerned about that because we knew the history of our group which had lost all its airplanes in that low-level mission earlier on in the war resulting in a change in tactics for the mediums. We were to bomb a town called Butzbach from 11,500 feet, then make a diving turn and strafe the town's railroad tracks. There were two flights. The lead flight was led by Squadron commander

Lt Colonel J B (Dirt Track) Smith, and the flight we were on was led by Major Sebille, the operations officer. We had to make a second bombing run as our lead bombardier, Fred Crandall, couldn't get lined up the first time. On the second run, we had seen the Colonel had been hit and gone down and we didn't know how many other airplanes had been hit down there. At the time that this was going on we were making our second run, I can literally remember praying to be hit because I knew at that altitude if I was hit I could jump, but down on the deck there wasn't anything you could do but bend over and kiss your ass good bye. In any event, Colonel Smith got on the wrong town. Instead of Butzbach, he hit Bad Nauheim and that turned out to be German General von **Rundstedt**'s headquarters, and they shot them down. I heard later from talk with one of the fellows that Sebille, who was our lead, had already told Smith whatever you do don't go straight in, be jinking back and forth. We flew on Sebille and he was literally just bouncing around, looked like something out of the movies. I remember his guns just flaming as we went through that town. Ours were hammering. I can also remember watching tracers which looked like they are just floating as they come up toward you and then when closer they just zip by. We were moving at red line speed of 350 miles per hour. We had also been told earlier by the Colonel that when we strafed he didn't mean at 50 feet, he meant on the deck. And we were almost kicking up dust as we went by. The idea was to strafe this town and then we were to climb up a little hill and wind around it. We were low. All of a sudden, a fellow by the name of Lyman went underneath us and went up the hill yelling, "Money on the bar and steers on the range." Lyman was from Wyoming and a cowboy. I asked him later, "how fast were you going?" and he said, "I think it was 420." That's about 70 miles an hour faster than the red line for that airplane which was 350. Probably an exaggeration. Don't know if that was true, but I do know he went under us like a scalded dog and went up the hill. At that time you couldn't go fast enough to suit me. Lyman was drowned after the war leading some steers across a river in Wyoming.

Post lowlevel raid PR shot

One of my very good friends, Jim Mossman from Philadelphia, flew as Colonel Smith's copilot that day because his usual copilot (De Rouen, who no one else would fly with) had a piece of flak that he had carried for a long time. It had migrated into his knee joint and he couldn't fly. So Mossman flew as the colonel's copilot and the whole crew went down, which was a seven man crew and carried the lead Bombardier, a guy by the name of Thibodeaux (sp?). After that I believe they had to lead DeRouen off. Lt. DeRouen had been in one bad crash and lived alone because no one else would live with him. He was the one who wouldn't cut his hair and the Colonel made him take names of people needing haircuts. Everyone in his tent had been killed and no one would move in with him. He was prone to sidle up to someone and tell you, "I think I know who will be next." We avoided him like the plague. He was an aspiring actor and used to go in to London when we were in England and have his picture made in all kinds of costumes. He was also proud of a scar he had received from the crash and announced that this would help him get character parts. He surely was one. I understand that he did eventually wind up in the film business. One of the fellows I worked with years later knew him and told me this.

Not all "low-levels" were in the air

As an aside, Major Sebille was a night club singer before the war; a prince of a fellow, and a tremendous pilot. He stayed in the Air Force after the war and was killed in Korea where he won the Congressional Medal of Honor. He got it posthumously because he was flying a P-51 when he told his wing man he had been hit. The wing man told him, "We can get back to the auxiliary field." Sebille told him, "It won't make any difference to me, I'm too badly hit." With that he took his P-51 right down on the deck and drove it straight into a Chinese convoy. Wiped the whole damn thing out and himself with it. And he did get the Congressional Medal.

Nice jacket (low level inheritance)

BOMB BAY LIFE

After some months in Beauvais we were ordered to move up to a field in Belgium near a town named Wavre. (This was immediately adjacent to Waterloo, made famous by Napoleon's defeat in 1815.)

I would be remiss if I did not mention the ground crew which we had. 1944 was one of the most severe winters which Europe had experienced in many years. These people kept those airplanes going regardless of battle damage, accidents, or weather. They were out there all night sweeping snow off the wings (without clear wings, aircraft will not fly). I have seen our crew chief run clean across the field once when we had come back early, He ran to see what was wrong. He also never hesitated to get in and fly with us to see if there was something wrong if we had reported some difficulty. I can't praise these ground crew people too highly as they were really the backbone of the Air Force. These men were not exactly young and in fact, some appeared to be middle aged but they were all experienced and all dedicated workers.

The cold winter exacerbated one of our "operations." Our outhouse which we referred to as "Hitler House" (because it had a picture of Hitler hanging up in it) was a four-holer type. It had no ends on it and not much front. Additionally, it was located adjacent to one of the hard stands for an airplane. There was nothing more exciting than to be there with "bomb bay doors open" when they ran up one of the airplanes and blew snow all through the thing; underneath it, on top of it and you.

On one raid that we flew very late in the war, we had been to before and we had to go back. This was a town in Germany called Wittenberg. There was a river there where the Germans had placed flak barges and as we flew into it the flak was truly intense. They were also shooting colored flak and I believe some phosphorous shells. Never knew what the colored flak was for unless it was to call fighters. The phosphorous shell put out long streamers of white and if they hit the airplane they stuck and burned. They also burned you if it got on you. This flak as I said was intense, and once we had bombed we were turning off the target and doing everything we could to get out of there. The whole flight, making a diving turn with everything fire walled, going as fast as we could go and when you do that you can easily overshoot the formation. At this time, Borst was flying, hands on throttles calling for max power. I was on the prop pitches because as we would start to overrun, I would jam the prop pitch forward turning the blade flat. This slowed the airplane to keep from over running the other airplanes but the increase in RPM made a terrible screaming noise. I don't recall our air speed but I imagine it was in the 300 mph range. We wanted out of there.

As previously stated, on occasion missions ran long, and for us a five-hour mission was a long mission. When it started in the afternoon, we might have to come back after dark. Coming back after dark with 36 airplanes is a challenge because we are all trying to get in, everybody's tired, running low on fuel and you are going to be landing in the dark. You still come over the field in sixes and then peel off in threes and then come in individually. We took off with a twenty-second interval between airplanes which would have three planes on the runway. If one aborted you knew there was one behind you and you had to pull-up to get over the aborter in front. At this time you relied on those 2000 HP engines and 13-foot, four-bladed props. It could seem that you were hanging on your props as you cleared the guy in front. You seemed to "walk over him." We could land with as close as an eight second interval before being waved off. There was a man in sort of a fox hole at the end of the runway that waved you off by firing a red flare when we were too close. An 8 second interval is truly close. Landing required the six ship flight coming over the 5000 foot runway at a thousand or twelve hundred feet. At the first end of the runway the lead three airplanes wheeled left (Right in some weather conditions) and the plane on the inside of the vee slipped under and became the third plane to land essentially in trail. The second three repeated this at the far end of the runway. This meant that the leader of the second vee was essentially, after turning on a short base leg, heading straight at the third plane from the first three who was approaching touchdown. It was then that the 8 second interval could occur.

Weather was always a problem; sometimes with snow and ice. Once when we were supposed to fly a mission, whoever was leading the group tried to get his airplane off the ground, went sailing down the runway with snow flying everywhere and at the end he had to abort because he couldn't get any lift. Also on occasion when we had ice, as you started off the airplane would literally slither from side to side slipping back and forth until you attained speed. Depending on where the snow was coming down or the weather was worse, we would take off and turn left or turn right to form up. Usually we went through an overcast in formation. When flying in formation and in the overcast, the lead climbs as straight as he can and you have got six airplanes there in formation all close enough that even in the densest fog you can see each other. Something in your inner ear I suppose always makes it appear after a while that the lead is turning when he is not. Hopefully you come through on top and haven't run into anyone. Sometimes they did interfere with each other and run into each other. Also the heavy bombers were usually high above us forming early in the morning in the dark and you could see them up there firing flares trying to form up a great formation of B-17s or 24's. It may be 25,000 feet and occasionally they would run together. About the only good thing I could say about the heavies forming up is occasionally something would happen and one would have to crash-land near our field. They had this heavy flying equipment, warm suits and everything else which we did not have and they sometimes gave theirs to us. Heavies were flying out of England.

Climbing through weather you could get into icing conditions although the only time I ever remember this I believe we were flying in a flight led by Smokey Smith. As we climbed ice formed up on the propellers and we were using the propeller de-icers. The ice slinging up against the side of the airplane made a racket.

Another hairy incident was when we had a hung bomb in the bomb bay. Each bomb was held in by two shackles, one at the front and one at the back. The bomb has a little propeller on the end of it, retained motionless by a safety wire. The propeller starts spinning up as the safety wire pulls and as the bomb drops the little spinning propeller arms the fuse so the bomb will explode on impact. This bomb was hanging nose down and obviously the wire which would retain that propeller had pulled and that propeller was spinning and the bomb was armed. We couldn't risk a landing with that bomb hanging there because it could drop from the airplane on landing impact and explode right under the airplane. David Foil, our flight engineer, went back into the bomb bay and standing on the cat walk with the bomb doors open below him fiddled with that bomb enough to get it loose and the bomb dropped and of course exploded when it hit. I don't know for sure but I believe he had to do this without his chute. As air crew he had a snap on chest type that could have prevented him from working on the bomb to free it. We didn't report this when we carne back as we should have. Foil should have been written up for a Distinguished Flying Cross. At that time we didn't pay much attention to it and really didn't even want to talk to the PR types that met the airplane to ask if there was anything to write up. We received an Air Medal for every five missions flown. I understand that some Groups were awarded a DFC for 25 missions. Not ours. [Foil **would receive the Distinguished Flying Cross 70 years later at a ceremony in Show Low, Arizona.—Ed.**]

I remember it being very, very cold and after a while you get so grungy and grimy that you have to do something. I took my steel helmet, built a fire underneath it and heated water, and standing buck naked in the snow at least got somewhat of a bath in order to stand myself. I only did that once and that was enough. From then on my helmet always had a burn mark on top of it where it had been sitting on a fire. This was my GI helmet. We all had one. But I also had a different type of flak helmet. Similar but it also had steel ear flaps.

The way the B-26 is built there is no way for the two pilots to easily bail out. The only possibility was going our through the bomb bay if the bomb bay doors are open or going out the nose wheel well which you could drop down right out through the bottom. You could not bail out through the two open hatches on top of the pilots' compartment because the propellers were behind you and if you bailed out there you would fly right in into the propellers. Also it was necessary for the copilot to push his seat back in an emergency to allow the bombardier to get out of the nose; otherwise he was in like a burglar. Another humorous thing (not too funny at the time) but finally in desperation, Foil, our Flight Engineer and myself cut each other's hair. David did not have a lot at all at the time and to this day claims that the reason he is bald now is because I cut his hair too short. My only recollection is pinching his ear with the scissors. I never could figure out how to do that without clipping the ear. But he nevertheless has always mentioned that I caused him to be bald.

To get the little fire started with these little potbellied stoves would go slip out to the hard stand at night and steal a little oil, and use that oil to kindle the fire. One night one of the fellows though had gone out in the dark and instead of getting oil he got gasoline out of a tank, not realizing. what he had. I remember I was walking down through the middle of the tents when I saw the top of the stove pipe lid fly up into the air and he ran out with his face and everything else on fire. The thing had exploded on the stove and blew flame all over him. He was gone for a long time to the hospital and finally came back to the squadron but he looked totally different. You would not have recognized him because he had been badly scarred by the fire.

An incident that pretty well limited any chance for advancement for me happened when a group of us had a birthday at about the same time. We all had a little bit too much except for Kiel, the Bombardier who did not drink. Everyone was feeling good and

Kiel wanted to get into the spirit of the thing. He went out back of the tent and fired his 45-automatic off seven times. Now even in World War II the Army looked poorly on people shooting pistols in Squadron areas. The next day around comes Major Root, the Adjutant (I shouldn't talk of him as he is dead now but he never was a winner) and Major Sebille, the Operations Officer investigating what had happened. I was sitting on my bunk when in walks Root and Sebille. Root of course was interrogating people and he looked at me and wanted to know what happened. I professed ignorance. He says, "Well who shot that pistol?" I said I didn't know. He then looked at me and said, "You're a liar Lieutenant." Well that really set the redneck in me off. At 20 or 21 you're easily "engaged." I stood up and was ready to go outside with him. And of course with that, Sebille, who was the Operations Officer (Root was what we called a paddle foot, i.e. non flying) pulled Root out; and the thing passed. I was quite angry because in reality I did know who shot the damned pistol and I was lying and that made me even madder. Kiel sat silent as the (Expletive Deleted) he was. Of course after several days Kiel went down and confessed to the   CO. Colonel Smith commended him, telling him what a fine fellow he was to come forward and shortly promoted this (E D again) to First Lieutenant. I was becoming a man who had been a Second Lieutenant so long I had green bars. Even after being checked out as pilot I couldn't quite figure out why I wasn't made a First Lieutenant because others did get promoted. However, when I got my fmal papers on discharge I noticed in my performance file Colonel Smith's signature where I had been rated Excellent (mandatory for promotion) had been struck out, struck through and overwritten VS which is Very Satisfactory which was the kiss of death. This was initialed by Root the day after Colonel Smith got killed. This pretty well followed me through the Army and to this day I hold it against Root, dead or not. It is interesting that he never came to any of the Squadron reunions because there were too many of the ground crew laying for him. But I tell everyone I was a commissioned officer with green bar rank. Actually I understand that I was eligible for promotion at discharge as a matter of procedure if you applied for it. Sort of a tombstone promotion. I never applied.

The field we flew out of in Beauvais was not the best. We had to go non-operational once for several days to try to fix the field. We had everybody working as a laborer out to try to do something with it. The field was so rough that I was told we only got about six landings on a set of tires before they got cut up and had to be replaced.

Flying a big airplane, and while a B-26 is not as big as a B-17, it nevertheless can be heavy on the controls. When you were flying formation, it's not exactly coordination, it's physical labor. This was before power assist. No matter how cold it is outside or in the cockpit, you can sweat like a stuck hog as you are literally doing physical labor holding formation. B26s had another peculiarity called rudder nibble. You were always feeling an indeterminate pressure one way or the other nibbling on the rudder pedals. Top turret gunner tracking exacerbated this. You can trim an airplane to where it will fly straight and level hands off, but I and some others kept it trimmed slightly off when in a wing position so that in the event you are hit it will throw you out of formation. Of course in No 4, the slot, there's no place to go.

We also got the feeling about now that this war was going to last forever and that it would never be over. You were going to be there until the war was over or you were dead. We had a tour of duty at that time for a medium bomber pilot of 65 missions. Fortunately the war got over after I had completed 42 missions. One of the funnier things that always struck me as funny was at a reunion once I met one of the fellows that had been shot down his first or second mission. This seemed bad to me as he was a POW for a long time and when he asked me how many missions I had I said 42. He said he couldn't imagine flying that many. I in turn couldn't imagine being a year or two in a prison camp.

After Colonel Smith was killed on the low level raid he was replaced by a Major Egan. We didn't know him and didn't know where he carne from and he did not immediately endear himself to us. First thing he decided was that everyone would fall out at daylight for physical training or exercise. He fell out with Major Root although no one else came out which ended that. Someone stole his damned jeep and wrecked it. He then made a bunch of us stand out in the snow and hold their shirt up because whoever wrecked it had gone over the steering wheel and he was looking at everybody's chest for marks to see who it was. Never did find him. He was also a little slow on starting evasive action after we crossed the bomb line. Them someone found it necessary to "clear his guns" and shoot those tracers under him. That started him.

About the only time I ever felt sorry for anybody in the German Air Force was at the bridge of Remagen. The Germans failed to blow it up and the allies were going across it in strength. The German's Stuka dive bombers were trying to bomb the thing. I could see them off to one side with a solid cloud of our anti-aircraft fire going up and these guys in these old Stukas were trying to dive bomb that bridge and knock it out. Don't know how any of them got through that flak but there they were trying their best anyway. Later story says Hitler executed the German officer that had failed to blow the bridge.

Sometimes flak comes up almost like magic and suddenly starts appearing around you. (That's why we wanted Egan to get on with the evasive action early. They usually fired a four-gun battery and they would go right by your wing tip just as you turned taking evasive action. Flak is an 88 mm shell, a rather large artillery projectile and can easily blow you out of the air. You can can smell it, you can see it, and you can hear it. As stated earlier when you are flying you can do evasive action and the whole flight and Group would be turning 15 left, 15 right, 30 left, 40 right and on and on. You are sort of jinking around trying to get out of it or avoid it. We assumed that we had about a second for every 1,000 feet of altitude so that meant at 11,500 in about 11 or 12 seconds they could be on you. Sometimes you could see it up ahead where you were going in although they usually tried to route us around flack belts where they knew it, but sometimes they didn't. Then you could look up ahead and see the people up ahead of you going through it and realize you were going to go through it too. In a way that reminds me of my age now. As you look up ahead you know you are 82 years old and you can see all that flak coming up and you've got to go through it and sooner or later one of them is going to hit you. Just hope it's quick because we're all flying without parachutes at this age.

I used to wonder if they would shoot at just one airplane. On one occasion we had engines not running as well as possible and we fell behind the Group. We were sitting ducks and an easy mark for fighters. Each time we would try to fly straight to catch the Group, the flak would come up on us and we had to start evasive action. We would fall further behind and then we would try to race to catch up. I don't remember whether Dewey was flying or I was, but as we rolled to the right there was an Me 109 just below and to the right getting ready to hose us down with his 20 mm cannons. As we rolled right apparently he realized that a B-26 has four package 50 guns, and thought we were going to shoot at him. He rolled away. That's the last we saw of him; not exactly a hero.

Our quarters in Belgium were probably the best I ever had in the Army. We were in a part of what had been an orphanage. We had one of the buildings with the kids and nuns in another almost adjoining. Only shortcoming was a church next door that rang its bells about three or four times an hour, night and day. Mess hall was on the first floor. Belgium being a small country seemed to have a sort of streetcar railway that took you anywhere you wanted to go. We were some distance from the air field and had to be trucked over to fly. I got in to Brussels on VE night. British soldiers everywhere really whooping it up. One memory is of a middle-aged man with a little boy. The lights had come on for the first time since the war started. He stopped me and said, "Thank you for this. My little boy has never seen these lights" and shook my hand.

When not flying and not on operations (we flew six days out of eight, six on and two off, unless there was a maximum effort and then everybody flew), we had time on our hands. You couldn't get off and go anywhere, although occasionally you could get a pass to a town, Beauvais, Louvain or wherever you were based but not often. We stood around most of the time talking, killing time, cleaning up gear, and we chunked knives at all the tress around. We were given a trench knife as part of our gear and I never quite knew why as I didn't plan on any knife fights with anyone. We also had a small crap table in the area. Some of the guys shot craps. I remember one short bombardier by the name of Pete Libby from South Philly who shot craps and never, never won. Invariably, he would get his pay and go and lose it all and then come back and beg and whine until he got maybe $10 from somebody, swearing he would never gamble again. He would then lose half of that which left him about $5 for rations. This happened month after month and was a standard joke.

One foolish thing that some guys did was to fly with just your flight boots. They were lined, warm, comfortable. and fit loosely. They were made, however, to fit over your GI shoes. If they had to jump the boots came off when the chute opened and they were left barefooted. This was no country to be barefooted. Winter was brutal.

One of the few times I ever won any money was playing Black Jack. I was waiting for mission to go off and it kept delaying and delaying and finally I got up to about $60-70. Of course you couldn't quit a game because it was pretty bad form and you really weren't allowed to quit if you were a big winner.

Before starting out we went out and checked the airplane over. Foil the Flight Engineer took a real good look at it and checked everything .back and forth. I had one superstition: I didn't want anyone to take my picture before I took off and I don't think I was the only one as there were a few pictures of guys that didn't make it back. It was sort of considered bad luck I thought. Everybody also took a chance to take one last pee because otherwise you could have to go in the airplane in a relief tubes in the pilots' compartment. There were none for anybody else. Nobody wanted to use those anyway and usually if you had to go you went out in the bomb bay and did your thing.

After a while in this environment of combat you just get sort of head down, dogged it and kept going. It seemed to be never ending. We did have a tour of duty to look forward to but the German Air Force had none. That wound up killing most of them. The British flew a tour of so many missions and when this was completed (how many I never knew) I think they got two weeks off.

One thing that I did learn that stood me very well later in life. We used to refer to some missions as a "maximum effort." All four squadrons in the group flew. Later, when I was working at Boeing and an executive would come through on a new project and tell everyone, "This is max effort, we're going all out," I would think to myself, buddy, you don't know what max-effort is. Max effort means your ass is on the line. Working hard and getting the job done is one thing but if there is a good chance you are not going to make it through the day, that's max effort and that's when you really turn on.

BELGIUM TO PENSACOLA (VIA VENLO)

We could sense the war winding down now. The Luftwaffe (German Air Force) was diminished although it still had teeth--witness the Battle of the Bulge. Flak, if anything was worse. Flying at this time was especially harrowing as no one wanted to be the last one shot down. My last mission recorded was on April 20th but I know we flew a little after that before VE Day which was May 8, 1945.

I was checked out as Pilot at our base in Belgium. Finally. Smith, our flight leader (the Smith from White River Junction in Vermont) checked me out in old No. 802, oldest plane in the squadron, name of *Pappy's Pram*, the one that never wanted to take off but flew like an angel (OK a little exaggeration) once off the ground. I remember Smith well as he borrowed my trench coat (pretty natty at the time), and also $20 to go on a pass. He left without returning either. Not much to do now but sign out and fly around when you wanted to. Enjoyable. Sometimes we would load up the airplane with 15 or so ground crew and fly around low over Germany and show them battle damage on the ground from about a thousand feet, occasionally lower. One city, Worms, was just holes in the ground. On one flight the tower advised that the wind had shifted to downwind for a landing but I could try it as they didn't think it was too bad. When I flared to land the thing sailed and didn't want to touch down. Fixed that by dumping flaps and we hit like a big chicken. Not really severe (I've ridden through worse commercially as well as others during the war), but it was a bouncer. The plane had hardly stopped before that bunch were abandoning ship. Don't know if any of them flew a sightseeing mission again.

We had moved up to Wavre in Belgium in the early Spring of '45. For some reason I rode up with a bunch in an army truck. Somewhere along the road in Flanders a bunch of guys bought cherries at a road side stand. Not me. They were green or something because this caused several stops to allow the unfortunate fruit lovers to look for a hoorah bush to hide behind for relief.

When we arrived in Belgium the war was still going on at a pretty good clip, winding down or not. One day we went in to briefing and there was a big red line drawn on the map. What's that? The Russians are somewhere behind that line, no one knew for sure, but do not cross and bomb anything on the other side. I didn't know it at the time but I guess that was really the start of the cold war.

VE Day (Victory in Europe) arrived and we were given passes to go into Brussels. British troops were almost rolling in the streets in joyous celebration. This was pretty much a British area. They had (allegedly) also drank up everything. One bartender offered a mixture of egg yellow and cognac. Passed on this. We had to eat British rations on one occasion and to this day I still think the mutton (Brit delicacy?) had hair on it. As an aside on a later trip to Brussels a group of us were sitting in a little cafe when this little fellow with a small black suitcase came in and opened it up to the proprietor. French discussion. I asked later what was going on and was told this was a black marketeer and he was selling pork chops. Must have been great as they were surely not refrigerated.

Fraternization with German girls was strictly forbidden. However about this time some of the fellows located a nearby lake where some girls had accumulated. Fraternization with the enemy began in earnest. Seems like discipline was not being maintained. I had just heard of this when the powers that be put out the word that German castrator mines were in that area. This pretty well stopped this activity and discipline was restored. This type of mine fires projectiles upward between your legs.

Don't remember if it was back in France or here in Belgium but passed a mob in the street throwing stuff, furniture and clothing, out the window. Outside they were holding a woman and had cut her hair off until she was almost bald. Said she was a collaborator and had taken up with the Germans.

At the end of the war, slightly after, actually, the 322nd was broken up. Crew dispersed. Borst, Kusluch and some others were sent into Germany to do something in the clean up. All I know is that that's where Kusluch was killed when he and a fellow named George Gaudette were flying a German trainer.

I was transferred to the 391st Group in Venlo, Holland. I remember again being back in a pyramidal tent. Hot weather, sandy soil, pine trees, not unlike my area in Florida. We were mixed in with their crews and mainly flew an occasional air show when we would fly down the Rhine to show off for some one. It was here that I guess I came close to a trip to the far east. I was dressed in a class A uniform getting ready to go into Venlo or somewhere when I was ordered to go over and familiarize myself with an A26 that was in the Group area for indoctrination purposes. This was replacing our B26s. They were widely used later in Korea. In fact out old Group Commander from the 322nd (Colonel Nye?) was killed in one in Korea when he flew in to a canyon at night and couldn't turn around. They were used for night intruder work there and one fellow that flew there said SOP was to drop a flare and if you could see it go down it meant that there was no mountain in the way so go on down. (I digress.) I went and sat in the cockpit for about an hour, reading the manual and was to fly it that afternoon or next day. You had to read about it as it didn't have a copilot and there was no way to get dual instruction. Right after that I was told to forget it. You have too many points, you're going home. (Points were awarded for time in theater, decorations and I don't know what else. I had 8 Air Medals and 5 Battle stars as well as a Distinguished Unit Citation).

Needless to say I was overjoyed. We were to be flown to England for processing. I got a ride with a crew I did not know in one of the 391st B26s. The pilot had his kid brother along who was visiting from some Army unit nearby. I rode (the only time) in the tail gunner's compartment. Cramped but good visibility. This pilot that I didn't know proceeded to show his kid brother "How we did it in combat." Scared me worse than combat. I was afraid that after surviving 42 missions I was to be another statistic. Finally made England and was quartered in a small house at a British Army prewar base known as Tidworth. About 6 or 8 of us in what I suppose had been a British Officer's family quarters. Mess hall was old army with trophies of England's past glory decorating the walls. Spears, flags etc. Waiters were usually Italian prisoners who were very pleasant and glad to be there. They seemed to be allowed to run free and usually tried to sell you a souvenir. I have a lighter from one of them, made from a crashed airplane's propeller. He assured me it was a German propeller. There were also German prisoners who seemed to get the heavy assignments. They were guarded and locked up at night.

Our house had a mixed bag with officers in it from all branches. Our senior officer was a Lt. Colonel from an Anti-Aircraft outfit. After staying there about a week or 10 days we were beginning to wonder why. Finally the Colonel went out looking for someone in charge. He came upon some kind of headquarters and was asked where are your headquarters people. When he told them we had none and were what you called casuals, the response was God Almighty we aren't set up for casuals, only units. We could have been there till yet I suppose. Thankfully we were soon shipped off to Southampton to go home on the *Queen Mary*. An 81000-ton ocean liner. We arrived at dark and I asked where is the ship. Right next to you. And there was that enormous black wall that was the side of the *Queen Mary*. Walking aboard was like entering the lobby of a hotel. Like other junior officers I was assigned as a deck officer over a small area and told to keep the aisles open. This had been used as a troop ship through the war and accommodated 15,000 troops. Half the enlisted personnel were in bunks about 10 rows high and the others sleeping on deck. (I have visited the

Queen Mary, now an attraction in Long Beach California. They have most of it right but the bunks were not as high as they were during our crossing.) We were welcomed as being in New York which they laughingly called it an NYC suburb. A four-day crossing followed. The Queen was so fast that it did not run in convoy as it was assumed to be able to outrun U-Boats as well as the early slow torpedoes. This it did. It was reported (and so cited in a plaque in Long Beach) that on a submarine alert in the North Atlantic while carrying the 15000 troops the Queen went all ahead full, about 30 or 35 knots. A British light cruiser, the *Curacao*, on one side tried to cross in front of the Queen and was cut in two. Cruiser loss 338. The limey telling me about it, in a heavy accent said, "Of course we couldn't stop." On one occasion the "Grey Ghost" as it was called carried over 16000 troops.

I also almost became one of the missing in trying to keep the aisles clear. The soldiers in the stack of bunks would often have the soldier in the top bunk get seasick. Over the side of his bunk on all below. Said offended immediately climbed out and went topside further crowding the deck (and aisles). On one occasion I had to enforce my deck officer authority and wake a sleeping soldier and tell him to get out of the aisle. We were carrying the remnants of an Infantry Division (36th?). This man rose up, all 9 feet of him, and in a menacing tone said "Why?" My recollection is I deserted my post. He went back to sleep (I was watching to make sure he didn't follow me). As an officer I was in a stateroom. Sounds good. It was for two people. We had 15 in there. They served two meals a day and we did get to eat in the dining room. Enlisted personnel ate in one of the empty swimming pools in shifts. The ship had life boats for only 8,000 people and knew that if sunk they could easily lose 10,000 people.

When we approached NYC there was a strike and the Queen's captain brought it in to dock unaided without tug assistance. We thought we would just step out on the dock. No, it takes time to unload 15,000 people. Took about a day and a half as I recall. We were put on ferries and transported across to Weehawken NJ. One of the guys on the ferry saw a tug run by his dad and jumped in and swam to it. When we walked through the ferry terminal I had one of my most memorable memories of the war. We must have looked pretty beat up. All carrying a large duffel bag on our shoulder and quietly shuffling to the busses. Then the civilians that I remember as older men, gray looking, started to applaud, and the whole dock took it up. For some reason this is and was an extremely emotional experience. No parades, none needed, I was home.

Busses took us to Camp Kilmer, a big milkshake and steak for dinner. (Steak was tough.) Only there a day or so and put on a train to Camp Blanding Florida. That's where I was discharged. Caught the bus home to Pensacola, got a cab and on a full moonlight night in November I got home about 4 AM. Had to knock to get in. It was over. Back in my bed room I remember feeling lonely as I had lived with a group of people for so long that it was unnatural. I was home unscathed although I guess I have a few brain scars. One of the lucky ones. No post-traumatic stress syndrome. Don't think that had been invented then. But for many months I carried what seemed like a weight on my back, sort of a feeling of dread. Couldn't shake the feeling that I was going to have to go back out and climb in and take off. Only two recurring nightmares that lasted for years. One was I was flying and watched the air speed indicator slow down to 150, needle shook and the airplane stalled, I was falling. Awakened with a rush. The other is not something I ever saw but had heard about after the three ship collision. An airplane had crashed and when I went over to it and opened a hatch a torrent of blood gushed out. I don't have these anymore.

The 322nd Bomb Group flew 425 combat missions in Northern Europe from May of 1943 to the war's end in May of '45. The Group had 763 casualties. Loss breakdown was 306 killed, 220 wounded, 156 missing, and 81 prisoners. Our loss rates were considered light, especially compared to the heavy bombers'. But high enough. Especially if you knew the casualty personally. As an aside there are still 72,000 missing from World War II. Some possibly clerical errors, others sank/drowned, burnt up, crash impact, dismembered, buried on impact or grave registration missed.

> They shall grow not old, as we that are left grow old:
> Age shall not weary them, nor the years condemn.
> At the going down of the sun and in the morning
> **We will remember them.**
> — Binyon, "For the Fallen" (1914)

From my enlistment in November 1942 I trained in some form or other until I left Lake Charles in an overseas movement on July 18th, 1944. Out of Dow Field, Maine on July 23rd, Presque Isle, Maine July 31st, Goose bay Labrador, August 1, Keflavik Iceland, August ?, Prestwick Scotland, August 13, Burtonwood England, August 14, over to Toomebridge, Ireland, and back reaching the 322nd in Great Saling England in early September. (Thanks to some notes of David Foil). First mission was in early Fall I believe. The rest is history.

> No destined anguish lifted its snaky head to poison
> a harmless young shepherd in a soldier's coat.
> —Blunden, Undertones of War (1928)

Ninth Air Force shoulder patch

According to the 314-page *Army Air Forces Statistical Digest of World War II*, published in December 1945 (https://apps.dtic.mil/dtic/tr/fulltext/u2/a542518.pdf), there were 121,867 air corps casualties, a third (40,061) killed in action. Training accidents and stateside crashes, which accounted for 21,583 of the 65,164 total aircraft losses during the war, added 15000 deaths to these totals.

A thousand shall fall at thy side, and ten thousand at thy right hand; but it shall not come nigh thee.

--Psalm 91:7

Survivor 0-715723
Margaret M. Cowart, Portrait of the Author, ca. 1950

ABOUT THE AUTHOR

Eugene G. Cowart

In 1942, still in his teens, Eugene Cowart left college to enlist as an aviation cadet in the US Army. The following recounts his experiences: training as a B26 bomber pilot at various stateside bases, flying the Atlantic at age nineteen, and joining his squadron to participate in forty-five missions over France, Germany, Belgium, and the Netherlands. He received five bronze battle stars, denoting participation in campaigns in Northern France, the Ardennes (Battle of  the Bulge), Rhineland, Central Europe, and Southern France. He also participated in Operation Clarion (22-23 February 1945), when massed allied aircraft flew almost 9000 sorties against German transportation centers to hasten the end of the war. His decorations included the Air Medal with one silver and three bronze oak leaf clusters, as well as a Distinguished Unit Citation and the European African Middle East Theater ribbon.

Leaving the service in September, 1945, he returned to college at the University of Alabama, where he took a B.S. in Engineering in 1948. Upon graduation, he embarked on an engineering career of over four decades, including work in oil, paper, and chemicals (the last involved managing a catalytic converter manufacturing facility and the global distribution of its product). His professional life reached its apogee, however, in some thirty years with the Boeing Company's aerospace projects (primarily in Seattle,

Washington and Huntsville, Alabama, but with months-long assignments in Florida and Southern California as well). He worked, early on, on military rockets and, later, on the Apollo program. He was Boeing's Chief Engineer in support of NASA's Lunar Roving Vehicle, which accompanied the final Apollo missions in 1971 and 1972.

When he retired in 1990, he was Chief Engineer of Boeing's Huntsville Division.

He considers the professional achievements secondary to his long and happy marriage. He and Margaret Irene Matthews were wed in 1946; their two children were born in 1947 and 1949. At the time of Margaret's death in 2011, they had been married sixty-five years.

He continues to reside in Huntsville. Not being promoted to first lieutenant still rankles.